Understanding 2 Timothy

Using Semitic Bible Study Methods with a new foundation

Michael Harvey Koplitz

Sandra Jean Koplitz

Table of Contents

Introduction

When a person is baptized as an infant and grows up in the church, their religious DNA assimilates different paradigms. The church has a message to give about Jesus Christ and His importance. Very few people study the theology and doctrines of the church to determine for themselves the accuracy of the church. The Proto-Orthodox church, which survived the pressures of the Roman Empire, decided to oppose any expression of Christianity that did not fit its dogma in its infancy. In addition, the Proto-Orthodox church would permanently destroy any writings that the rival Christians had developed.

The Gnostic Christians of Northern Egypt viewed the life of Jesus of Nazareth in a completely different way than the Proto-Orthodox church did. They saw the message about the Kingdom of Heaven as the vital purpose of Jesus. His birth, death, and resurrection are not mentioned in the Gnostic Gospels. However, did the Proto-Orthodox church destroy the Gnostic Gospels when they crushed said movement? The answer is yes and no. Yes, they destroyed what they got their hands on. No, because in 1948, copies of the Gnostic religious books were discovered in Alexandria, Egypt. Once these documents were translated, the world learned what the Gnostic Christians believed. It is fascinatingly different than what the Proto-Orthodox said about these followers of Christ.

Why is this understanding critical? Much research points to a different situation in the early years than what the church espouses. A lot of this information is available to anyone today. However, the Seminaries and churches will not openly discuss these other writings about Jesus and His disciples. The scholars teaching in most Seminaries have learned their lessons from the church and closed-minded mentors who refuse to look at other possibilities. This is because the Western European world took Christianity and changed it from a Near Eastern religion to Western religion.

There is a theory that Paul converted Mithras House Churches into Jesus House Churches. This is clear from the connection between the Mithras' and Christianity's rituals. For example, baptism was the initiation ritual of Mithras. Communion did not originate with Jesus. This ritual was a part of Mithras, where the followers would share his flesh (bread) and drink his blood (wine). There are many more rituals that Christianity picked up from Mithras. A good reference is "Christianity's Need for Mithras," which the author wrote.

Did Paul create the churches in the letters he sent, which comprise the New Testament, and if so, they must have been Jewish groups who became Jewish Christians? They would have continued with their Hebraic rituals and saw Jesus of Nazareth as the Messiah that the prophets of old had promised. They would have adopted many of Jesus' teachings and tried to live by them. The letters in the New Testament are written in Greek. However, most Jews in the Roman Empire did not speak Greek; instead, they spoke Aramaic and Hebrew. These congregations would not have understood a Greek letter from Paul.

Therefore, the letters in the New Testament must have been written in Aramaic and then transliterated into Greek. The same can be said for the Gospels, all of them. The church, over the centuries, decided who wrote the Gospels and their intent. The only Gospel we can assign to a writer is Luke. The other three are up in the air about who wrote them. While in Seminary, the author was taught that the entire New Testament was originally written in Koine Greek. However, that raised the question, "Did Jesus speak Greek?" The Seminary instructors said, "no, Jesus did not speak Greek." Then the New Testament, especially the Gospels, must have been written in Aramaic. After all, Jesus spoke Aramaic and Hebrew.

We know this because He was a poor *tekton* (a stonemason or carpenter) from an impoverished city named Nazareth. Being born to a Jewish family in Galilee, he would have learned the traditions of His people and trade. He would have learned to speak Aramaic, the language of the area. He would have learned Hebrew because that was the language of the synagogue and the Temple in Jerusalem. In other words, Hebrew was the language of God, and Jewish males learned the language.

Suppose you are ready to toss this manuscript into the nearest trash can or delete it off your electronic device at this point in the introduction. In that case, the writer has your attention. This is the reaction when the writer has spoken with persons who had been indoctrinated into the church's position since birth. The author did not come into the church environment until he was 35. Therefore, the church's paradigms, dogma, and doctrine were not a part of his DNA. Instead, he questioned a lot. He found many inconsistencies between the Bible and the doctrines of the church. Seminary was an experience to learn what the church had evolved into two-thousand years after the death of Jesus.

There are more parts to the premise that the New Testament was originally written in Aramaic and will be explored. For the reader to grasp the subsequent phases of the proof, an open mind is critical.

Culture and Language

Let us continue in the journey of examining the New Testament to determine its original language. Nothing in stone tells us that Aramaic is the Original Language of the New Testament. However, nothing says that Koine Greek was the original language of the New Testament either. Therefore, we have two theories about the original language of the New Testament. The author admits that the Seminary he attended drove home the belief that the Old Testament was written in Hebrew, except for a few spots. The New Testament was initially written in Koine Greek.

The writers' research has been searching for the original meaning of Scripture for many years. The methodology for this work is called "Ancient Bible Study Methods." The method was developed by Dr. Anne Davis of the Bible Learning University in Albuquerque, New Mexico. The author studied this method with Dr. Davis as his mentor. It became clear that the search for the original meaning of the Scriptures requires that the culture and language be examined. So, the author's methodology is Dr. Davis' work, plus his Ph.D. studies combining the method, culture, and language.

The language examination is easy for the Old Testament because it was written in Hebrew, and about one-half of Daniel is in Aramaic. It does not take long to realize that idioms and figures of speech in the Hebrew of the Old Testament revealed a lot about the people and situation of the day when the scrolls were written. The Targums were a valuable resource because they are the Aramaic translations the rabbis did for the people living outside of Judea. The rabbis added commentary to the Targums because they knew that some of the idioms and speech used in the Near East would not translate well into the different areas where the Jews lived.

The culture of the Near East has been essentially the same in many aspects since the days of Jesus. Many practices of Jesus' day are still in use today. The culture of the Jews of the Near East is built into the language. Often an Aramaic or Hebrew word has a deep meaning that is only fully understood by natives living in that culture. The Old Testament is filled with cultural items that do not need to be spelled out because the people knew their culture in the author's time.

Suppose the New Testament in Koine Greek is a transliteration of the Aramaic. The culture, figures of speech, and idioms will be easily identified when examining the Peshitta (the Aramaic version of the New Testament). Indeed many of the so-called difficult words of Jesus are not tricky when examined in the light of the culture of Jesus' day. An example is "faith to move a mountain," Jesus said these words to His disciples. The church determined that this meant complete faith in Jesus. From the western European Greek point of view, that makes sense. What else could it possibly mean?

"Faith to move a mountain" is an Aramaic idiomatic expression. What Jesus said to His followers when he said this is that his disciples needed to be faithful so that they could change the "government's view through their words." The governing body for Judaism resided on the top of a mountain. Jerusalem, with its Temple, was built on the top of Mount Zion, a very tall mountain. This idiom survived because the Aramaic Gospels were transliterated into Koine Greek. Numerous other examples support this position.

Suppose the culture and language idioms of Jesus' day can be found in the Koine Greek because it was transliterated. In that case, it supports the theory of the Aramaic versions being the original language of the Gospels and possibly even more.

The Aramaic Version of the New Testament

The Peshitta is the accepted Aramaic translation of the New Testament for many churches of the East. Peshitta means "simple, true, direct, and original." It is a collection of scrolls that were compiled in 150 CE. There were some revisions to the Peshitta in the fifth and sixth centuries. The Greek version of the New Testament is a transliteration of the Peshitta.[1]

For centuries, the Catholic church has used the Latin version of the Bible, the Vulgate, and still uses it. The Vulgate was developed around 350 CE by Jerome by order of the Pope at that time. Erasmus (1466 – 1536) was the person who put together the Greek New Testament for the Catholic church.

"The New Testament, brought to light in the original Greek tongue, was compiled and made available for humanity to study and learn. Although working under and deeply associated with the Roman Catholic Church, the learned scholar declared his disagreement with those who wanted to keep the Scriptures from the common people. He said, "If only the farmer would sing something from them at his plow, the weaver moves his shuttle to their tune, the traveler lighten the boredom of his journey with Scriptural stories!" Little did he know that the work he was about to produce would change the world forever. This Greek New Testament, in printed form, would become the standard of the New Testament, launching the translations of Martin Luther and William Tyndale into the world. Thus, fulfilling his dream that all men would read the

---

[1] Rocco A. Errico and George M. Lamsa, *Aramaic Light on Galatians through Hebrews: A Commentary Based on Aramaic, the Language of Jesus, and Ancient near Eastern Customs* (Smyrna, GA: Noohra Foundation, 2005).

Bible for themselves in their common language. His new "study Bible" had two main parts, the Greek text, and a revised Latin edition, which was more elegant and accurate than the traditional translation of Jerome's Latin Vulgate. Erasmus prefaced this monumental work of scholarship with an exhortation to Bible study. He proclaimed that the New Testament contains the "philosophy of Christ," simple and accessible teaching with the power to transform lives."[2]

The church recognized Erasmus' Greek New Testament in 1515 CE. The church in the Near East has been using the Peshitta as the original language of the New Testament since 150 CE. If the Greek New Testament was important to the church as an original language, then why did it adopt the Vulgate in 350 CE? The church should have adopted the Greek New Testament at the beginning.

The Peshitta, translated into English, is used to examine Paul's letters. The rest of the methodology that the author developed for Ancient Bible Study Methods is the framework of this research.

---

[2] "Erasmus Greek New Testament," Insight of the King, accessed February 18, 2022, https://www.insightoftheking.com/erasmus-greek-new-testament.html.

The Messianic Tradition Change

One problem for Peter and the Disciples was that they claimed Yeshua to be the Messiah that the prophets of the Hebrew Scriptures spoke. However, Yeshua did not do what these traditions said. The main tradition was that the Messiah would destroy oppressive Romans and reinstate the Kingdom of Israel. Yeshua would then be declared the king and sit on David's throne in Jerusalem. That did not occur.

None of the messianic traditions of the day worked. So, what was the new movement going to do? They turned to the prophets and discovered Isaiah 50-53. These chapters are referred to as the Suffering Servant chapters. The Yeshua movement decided that the Suffering Servant was Yeshua. The portrayal of Yeshua's life does fit the Suffering Servant chapters. However, rabbinical interpretation then and now sees the Suffering Servant as the nation of Israel. Indeed, these chapters do describe the history of Israel. Nations have wanted to destroy the Jewish people since the time of Abraham.

The diaspora from the Babylonia Exile and the Assyrian invasions looked to squelch the Jewish people. The LORD promised that a remnant of the people would always survive. That is true throughout the 4,000-year history of the Jewish people. Many nations tried to destroy them, and the LORD intervened to ensure that a remnant of the people survived.

Paul must have been convinced in his encounter with Yeshua on the Damascus road that Yeshua was the Suffering Servant. It is clear from Paul's writings that he did believe this. For Paul, the Messiah was the Spiritual Messiah that the Kabbalah spoke. The

Kabbalah says that there will be two Messiahs. This theology is based on Zachariah 9:9. The first Messiah is Messiah ben Joseph. This Messiah was to restore the Kingdom of Heaven, a spiritual Kingdom. The second Messiah will be Messiah ben David. This Messiah was to restore the Kingdom of Israel. The Midrash from the Kabbalah did not state that the Messiah was two different souls.

The Kabbalah

There is a large amount of material in print about the Kabbalah. The Kabbalah referred to is Moses's Secret Work from Mount Sinai. Legends say Moses received three items on Mount Sinai when he met the LORD. The first is the written law. The written law is called the Torah. The second is the oral law. The oral law was put into a written form around 200 CE called the Mishnah. The third is the secret law called the Kabbalah. The secrets of the Kabbalah are based on the Torah and were written down around 200 CE. The main books of the Kabbalah are the Zohar and the Book of Creation.

Many of Yeshua's statements have Kabbalah undertones. Yeshua would have known the Kabbalah. Paul would have known the basics, at least, of the Kabbalah because of his religious education and training.

There are Kabbalistic ideas in the Gospels and Paul's letters. Kabbalistic verses will be highlighted in the chapters of the letters.

Methodology

The methodology employed is to use "Ancient Bible Study Methods" integrated with Jesus's day's customs and culture to examine the Hebrew and Christian Scriptures, thus gathering a more in-depth understanding by learning the Scriptures in the way the people of Jesus's day did.

I have titled the methodology of analyzing a passage of Scripture in a Hebraic manner the "Process of Discovery." The author developed this methodology, which combines various linguistic and cultural understanding areas. There are several sections to the process, and not all the parts apply to every passage of Scripture. The overall result of developing this process is to give the reader a framework for studying the Word in more depth.

The "Process of Discovery" starts with a Scripture passage. An examination of the linguistic structure of the passage is next. The linguistic structure includes parallelism, chiastic structures, and repetition. Formatting the passage in its linguistic form allows the reader to visualize what the first-century CE listener was hearing. Their corresponding sections label the chiasms, for example, A, B, C, B', A.' Not all passages of the Scriptures have a poetic form.

The next step is to "question the narrative." The narrative process of questioning the narrative assumes the reader knows nothing about the passage. Therefore, the questions go from simple to complex. The next task is to identify any linguistic patterns. Linguistic patterns include, but are not limited to, irony, simile, metaphor, symbolism, idioms, hyperbole, figurative language, personification, and allegory.

A review of any translation inconsistencies discovered between the English NAU version and Hebrew or Greek versions is done. Sometimes, a Hebrew or Greek word is translated in more than one way. Inconsistencies also can be created by the translation committee, which may have decided to use traditional language instead of the actual translation. The decision of the translation committee is in the Preface or Introduction to the Bible. Perhaps some of the inconsistencies were intentionally added to convey some deeper meaning. An examination of every discrepancy is done.

The passage is analyzed for any echoes of the Hebrew Scriptures in the Christian Scriptures. An echo occurs using a passage from the Hebrew Scriptures in the Christian Scriptures.[3] Also, echoes are found when Torah (Genesis through Deuteronomy) passages are used in other Hebrew Bible books. Cross-references in the Scripture are references from one verse to another verse, which can help the reader understand the verse.

The names of persons mentioned in the passage are listed. Many Hebrew names have meaning and may be associated with places or actions. Jewish parents used to name their children based on what they felt God had in store for their children. An example is Abraham, whose original name was Abram and was changed to mean eternal father (God changed Abram's name to Abraham, indicating a function he was to perform). When the Hebrew Bible gives names, many occurrences mean something unique. The same importance can occur for the names of places. The time it takes to travel between locations can supply insight into the event.

---

[3] Mitzvot are the 613 commandments found in the Torah that please God. There are positive and negative commandments. The list was first development by Maimonides. The full list can be found at: ttp://www.jewfaq.org/613.htm.

Keyphrases are identified in verses when they are essential to understanding that passage. There are no rules for selecting the keywords. Searching for other occurrences of the keywords in Scripture in concordance is necessary to understand the Word's usage; this must be done in either Hebrew or Greek, not in English. A classic Hebraic approach is to find the usage of a word in the Scripture by finding other verses that contain the Word. The usage of a word in its original language is discovered by searching the Scripture in the language of the Word. Verses that contain the Word are identified, and a pattern for the usage of the Word is discovered. Each verse is examined to see what the usage of the Word is, which may reveal a model for the Word's usage. The first usage of the Word in the Scripture, primarily if used in the Torah, is essential for Hebrew words. The Christian Scriptures are used for Greek words to determine the Word usage in the Scripture. Sometimes, finding the equivalent Greek Word in the Septuagint can be beneficial as analyzing its Hebrew usage.

The Rules of Hillel are used when applicable. Hillel was a Torah scholar who lived shortly before Jesus' day. Hillel developed several rules for Torah students to interpret the Scriptures, which refer to halachic Midrash. In several cases, these rules are helpful in the analysis of the Scripture.

The cultural implications from the writing period are done after the linguistic analysis is completed. The culture is crucial because it is not explicitly referenced in the biblical narratives, as indicated earlier.

From the linguistic analysis and the cultural understanding, it is possible to obtain a deeper meaning of the Scripture beyond the plain text's literal meaning. That is what the listeners of Jesus's time were doing. They put linguistics and culture together without even having to contemplate it.

The analysis will lead to findings explaining the passage's meaning in Jesus's day. Most of the time, the Hebraic analysis leads to the desire for more in-depth analysis to fully understand what Jesus was talking about or what was happening to Him. Whatever the result, a new, more in-depth understanding of the Scripture is obtained.

The components of the Process of Discovery are:

Language

Process of Discovery

Linguistics Section

Linguistic Structure

Discussion

Questioning the Passage

Verse Comparison of citations or proof text

Translation Inconsistencies

Biblical Personalities

Biblical Locations

Phrase Study

Linguistic Echoes

Rules of Hillel

Culture Section

Discussion

Questioning the passage

Cultural Echoes

Culture and Linguistics Section

Discussion

Thoughts

Only the applicable sections are included in this document.

Introduction to the Letter – 2 Timothy

"2 Timothy" is one of the books in the New Testament of the Christian Bible. It is traditionally attributed to the Apostle Paul and is addressed to Timothy, a young Christian leader and companion of Paul. The letter is believed to have been written from prison, during Paul's second Roman imprisonment, shortly before his execution.

The primary purpose of 2 Timothy is to encourage and instruct Timothy in his ministry, emphasizing the importance of remaining faithful to the teachings of Christ despite challenges and opposition. Paul also reflects on his own life and ministry, offering Timothy guidance on leadership, perseverance, and the importance of sound doctrine.

Throughout the letter, Paul emphasizes the need for endurance, faithfulness, and boldness in proclaiming the Gospel message. He urges Timothy to guard the truth, avoid false teachings, and continue in the faith that he has learned from Paul.

Key themes in 2 Timothy include:

1. Endurance and Perseverance: Paul encourages Timothy to remain steadfast in the face of difficulties and persecution.

2. Sound Doctrine: Paul emphasizes the importance of teaching and adhering to the true teachings of the Gospel, warning against false teachings and doctrines.

3. Leadership and Ministry: Paul provides guidance to Timothy on leadership qualities, responsibilities, and the conduct expected of a faithful servant of Christ.

4. Faithfulness and Boldness: Timothy is urged to continue in the faith and to boldly proclaim the Gospel message, regardless of opposition or personal challenges.

5. The Legacy of Paul: Paul reflects on his own life and ministry, encouraging Timothy to follow his example and to continue in the traditions passed down to him.

Overall, 2 Timothy serves as a poignant and personal letter from Paul to his beloved disciple, urging him to remain faithful and steadfast in his Christian faith and ministry, even in the midst of trials and difficulties. It continues to be a source of inspiration and guidance for Christians today.

Chapter One

Language

Peshitta	New American Standard 1995
2Timothy 1:1 Paul, a legate of Jesus the Messiah by the pleasure of God, according to the promise of life which is in Jesus the Messiah; **2** to Timothy a beloved son; grace, and mercy, and peace, from God the Father, and from our Lord Jesus the Messiah. **3** I thank God, whom I serve from my forefathers with a pure conscience, that I continually remember thee in my prayers, by night and by day: **4** and I desire to see thee, and I call to mind thy tears; that I may be filled with joy, **5** by the recollection which I have, by thy genuine faith, which dwelt first in thy grandmother Lois, and in thy mother Eunice, and also, I am persuaded, in thee. **6** Wherefore I remind thee, that thou excite the gift of God, that is in thee by the imposition of my hands. **7** For God hath not given us a spirit of fear, but of energy, and of love, and of instruction. **8** Therefore be not thou ashamed of the testimony of our Lord, nor of me his prisoner; but endure evils in connection with the Gospel, through the power of God; **9** who hath vivified us, and called us with a holy calling; not according to our works, but according to his good pleasure, and his grace that was given us in Jesus the Messiah from time before the ages, **10** and is now made known by the appearing of our Vivifier, Jesus the Messiah; who hath abolished death, and hath made manifest life and immortality, by the gospel: **11** of	**2Timothy 1:1** Paul, [a]an apostle of [b]Christ Jesus [1b]by the will of God, according to the promise of [d]life in Christ Jesus, **2Timothy 1:2** To [a]Timothy, my beloved [1b]son: [c]Grace, mercy *and* peace from God the Father and Christ Jesus our Lord. **2Timothy 1:3** [a]I thank God, whom I [b]serve with a [c]clear conscience [1]the way my forefathers did, [d]as I constantly remember you in my [2]prayers night and day, **4** [a]longing to see you, [b]even as I recall your tears, so that I may be filled with joy. **5** [1]For I am mindful of the [a]sincere faith within you, which first dwelt in your grandmother Lois and [b]your mother Eunice, and I am sure that *it is* in you as well. **6** For this reason I remind you to kindle afresh [a]the gift of God which is in you through [a]the laying on of my hands. **7** For God has not given us a [a]spirit of [1]timidity, but of power and love and [2]discipline. **2Timothy 1:8** Therefore [a]do not be ashamed of the [b]testimony of our Lord or of me [c]His prisoner, but join with *me* in [d]suffering for the [e]gospel according to the power of God, **9** who has [a]saved us and [b]called us with a holy [c]calling, [d]not according to our works, but according to His own [b]purpose and grace which was granted us in [e]Christ Jesus from [f]all

which I am constituted a herald and a legate, and a teacher of the Gentiles. **12** Therefore I suffer these things: and I am not ashamed; for I know in whom I have believed, and I am persuaded that he is competent to keep for me my deposit against that day. **13** Let the form of sound words, which thou hast heard from me, abide with thee; with faith and love, in Jesus the Messiah. **14** Keep thou the good deposit, by the Holy Spirit who dwelleth in us. **15** This thou knowest, that all those in Asia have turned from me; and that among them are Phygellus and Hermogenes. **16** May our Lord bestow mercy on the house of Onesiphorus; for, many times, he refreshed me, and was not ashamed of the chains of my imprisonment. **17** But also, when he came to Rome, he sought for me with diligence, and found me. **18** May our Lord grant him, that he may find mercy with our Lord, in that day. And how he ministered to me at Ephesus, thou very well knowest.

eternity, **10** but *a*now has been revealed by the *b*appearing of our Savior *c*Christ Jesus, who *d*abolished death and brought life and immortality to light through the gospel, **11** *a*for which I was appointed a preacher and an apostle and a teacher. **12** For this reason I also suffer these things, but *c*I am not ashamed; for I know *b*whom I have believed and I am convinced that He is able to *c*guard what I have entrusted to Him [1]until *d*that day. **13** [1a]Retain the *b*standard of *c*sound words *d*which you have heard from me, in the *e*faith and love which are in *f*Christ Jesus. **14** Guard, through the Holy Spirit who *a*dwells in us, the [1b]treasure which has been entrusted to *you.*

2Timothy 1:15 You are aware of the fact that all who are in [1a]Asia *b*turned away from me, among whom are Phygelus and Hermogenes. **16** The Lord grant mercy to *a*the house of Onesiphorus, for he often refreshed me and *b*was not ashamed of my [1c]chains; **17** but when he was in Rome, he eagerly searched for me and found me — **18** the Lord grant to him to find mercy from the Lord on *a*that day — and you know very well what services he rendered at *b*Ephesus.

2Timothy 1:1
[1]Lit *through*
[a]2 Cor 1:1
[b]Gal 3:26
[c]1 Cor 1:1
[d]1 Tim 6:19

2Timothy 1:2
[1]Or *child*
[a]Acts 16:1; 1 Tim 1:2
[b]1 Tim 1:2; 2 Tim 2:1; Titus 1:4
[c]Rom 1:7

2Timothy 1:3
[1]Lit *from my forefathers*
[2]Or *petitions*
[a]Rom 1:8
[b]Acts 24:14
[c]Acts 23:1; 24:16; 1 Tim 1:5
[d]Rom 1:9

2Timothy 1:4
[a]2 Tim 4:9, 21
[b]Acts 20:37

2Timothy 1:5
[1]Lit *Receiving remembrance of*
[a]1 Tim 1:5
[b]Acts 16:1; 2 Tim 3:15

2Timothy 1:6
[a]1 Tim 4:14

2Timothy 1:7
[1]Or *cowardice*
[2]Or *sound judgment*
[a]John 14:27; Rom 8:15

2Timothy 1:8

[a]Mark 8:38; Rom 1:16; 2 Tim 1:12, 16
[b]1 Cor 1:6
[c]Eph 3:1; 2 Tim 1:16
[d]2 Tim 2:3, 9; 4:5
[e]2 Tim 1:10; 2:8

2Timothy 1:9
[a]Rom 11:14
[b]Rom 8:28ff
[c]Rom 11:29
[d]Eph 2:9
[e]2 Tim 1:1
[f]Rom 16:25; Eph 1:4; Titus 1:2

2Timothy 1:10
[a]Rom 16:26
[b]2 Thess 2:8; 2 Tim 4:1, 8; Titus 2:11
[c]2 Tim 1:1
[d]1 Cor 15:26; Heb 2:14f

2Timothy 1:11
[a]1 Tim 2:7

2Timothy 1:12
[1]Or *for*
[a]2 Tim 1:8, 16
[b]Titus 3:8
[c]1 Tim 6:20; 2 Tim 1:14
[d]1 Cor 1:8; 3:13; 2 Tim 1:18; 4:8

2Timothy 1:13
[1]Or *Hold the example*
[a]2 Tim 3:14; Titus 1:9
[b]Rom 2:20; 6:17
[c]1 Tim 1:10
[d]2 Tim 2:2
[e]1 Tim 1:14
[f]2 Tim 1:1

2Timothy 1:14
[1]Lit *good deposit*

[a]Rom 8:9
[b]1 Tim 6:20; 2 Tim 1:12

2Timothy 1:15
[1]I.e. the province of Asia
[a]Acts 2:9
[b]2 Tim 4:10, 11, 16

2Timothy 1:16
[1]Lit *chain*
[a]2 Tim 4:19
[b]2 Tim 1:8
[c]Eph 6:20

2Timothy 1:18
[a]1 Cor 1:8; 3:13; 2 Tim 1:12; 4:8
[b]Acts 18:19; 1 Tim 1:3

2Timothy 1:1 Παῦλος, ἀπόστολος Ἰησοῦ χριστοῦ διὰ θελήματος θεοῦ, κατ᾽ ἐπαγγελίαν ζωῆς τῆς ἐν χριστῷ Ἰησοῦ, **2** Τιμοθέῳ ἀγαπητῷ τέκνῳ· χάρις, ἔλεος, εἰρήνη ἀπὸ θεοῦ πατρὸς καὶ χριστοῦ Ἰησοῦ τοῦ κυρίου ἡμῶν.

2Timothy 1:3 Χάριν ἔχω τῷ θεῷ, ᾧ λατρεύω ἀπὸ προγόνων ἐν καθαρᾷ συνειδήσει, ὡς ἀδιάλειπτον ἔχω τὴν περὶ σοῦ μνείαν ἐν ταῖς δεήσεσίν μου νυκτὸς καὶ ἡμέρας, **4** ἐπιποθῶν σε ἰδεῖν, μεμνημένος σου τῶν δακρύων, ἵνα χαρᾶς πληρωθῶ, **5** ὑπόμνησιν λαμβάνων τῆς ἐν σοὶ ἀνυποκρίτου πίστεως, ἥτις ἐνῴκησεν πρῶτον ἐν τῇ μάμμῃ σου Λωΐδι καὶ τῇ μητρί σου Εὐνίκῃ, πέπεισμαι δὲ ὅτι καὶ ἐν σοί. **6** Δι᾽ ἣν αἰτίαν ἀναμιμνήσκω σε ἀναζωπυρεῖν τὸ χάρισμα τοῦ θεοῦ, ὅ ἐστιν ἐν σοὶ διὰ τῆς ἐπιθέσεως τῶν χειρῶν μου. **7** Οὐ γὰρ ἔδωκεν ἡμῖν ὁ θεὸς πνεῦμα δειλίας, ἀλλὰ δυνάμεως καὶ ἀγάπης καὶ σωφρονισμοῦ. **8** Μὴ οὖν ἐπαισχυνθῇς τὸ μαρτύριον τοῦ κυρίου ἡμῶν, μηδὲ ἐμὲ τὸν δέσμιον αὐτοῦ· ἀλλὰ συγκακοπάθησον τῷ εὐαγγελίῳ κατὰ δύναμιν θεοῦ, **9** τοῦ σώσαντος ἡμᾶς καὶ καλέσαντος κλήσει ἁγίᾳ, οὐ κατὰ τὰ ἔργα ἡμῶν, ἀλλὰ κατ᾽ ἰδίαν πρόθεσιν καὶ χάριν τὴν δοθεῖσαν ἡμῖν ἐν χριστῷ Ἰησοῦ πρὸ χρόνων αἰωνίων, **10** φανερωθεῖσαν δὲ νῦν διὰ τῆς ἐπιφανείας τοῦ σωτῆρος ἡμῶν Ἰησοῦ χριστοῦ, καταργήσαντος μὲν τὸν θάνατον, φωτίσαντος δὲ ζωὴν καὶ ἀφθαρσίαν διὰ τοῦ εὐαγγελίου, **11** εἰς ὃ ἐτέθην ἐγὼ κῆρυξ καὶ ἀπόστολος καὶ διδάσκαλος ἐθνῶν. **12** Δι᾽ ἣν αἰτίαν καὶ ταῦτα πάσχω, ἀλλ᾽ οὐκ ἐπαισχύνομαι· οἶδα γὰρ ᾧ πεπίστευκα, καὶ πέπεισμαι ὅτι δυνατός ἐστιν τὴν παραθήκην μου φυλάξαι εἰς ἐκείνην τὴν ἡμέραν. **13** Ὑποτύπωσιν ἔχε ὑγιαινόντων λόγων ὧν παρ᾽ ἐμοῦ ἤκουσας, ἐν πίστει καὶ ἀγάπῃ τῇ ἐν χριστῷ Ἰησοῦ. **14** Τὴν καλὴν παραθήκην φύλαξον διὰ πνεύματος ἁγίου τοῦ ἐνοικοῦντος ἐν ἡμῖν.

2Timothy 1:15 Οἶδας τοῦτο, ὅτι ἀπεστράφησάν με πάντες οἱ ἐν τῇ Ἀσίᾳ, ὧν ἐστιν Φύγελος καὶ Ἑρμογένης. **16** Δώῃ ἔλεος ὁ κύριος τῷ Ὀνησιφόρου οἴκῳ· ὅτι πολλάκις με ἀνέψυξεν, καὶ τὴν ἅλυσίν μου οὐκ ἐπαισχύνθη, **17** ἀλλὰ γενόμενος ἐν Ῥώμῃ, σπουδαιότερον ἐζήτησέν με καὶ εὗρεν _ **18** δώῃ αὐτῷ ὁ κύριος εὑρεῖν ἔλεος παρὰ κυρίου ἐν ἐκείνῃ τῇ ἡμέρᾳ _ καὶ ὅσα ἐν Ἐφέσῳ διηκόνησεν, βέλτιον σὺ γινώσκεις.

Language

Process of Discovery

Linguistics Section

Linguistic Structure

[Introduction] 1 Paul, *ᵃ*an apostle of *ᵇ*Christ Jesus *¹*by the will of God, according to the promise of *ᵈ*life in Christ Jesus, **2** To *ᶜ*Timothy, my beloved *¹ᵇ*son: *ᶜ*Grace, mercy *and* peace from God the Father and Christ Jesus our Lord.

[Greeting] 3 *ᵃ*I thank God, whom I *ᵇ*serve with a *ᶜ*clear conscience *¹*the way my forefathers did, *ᵈ*as I constantly remember you in my *²*prayers night and day, **4** *ᵃ*longing to see you, *ᵇ*even as I recall your tears, so that I may be filled with joy. **5** *¹*For I am mindful of the *ᵃ*sincere faith within you, which first dwelt in your grandmother Lois and *ᵇ*your mother Eunice, and I am sure that *it is* in you as well. **6** For this reason I remind you to kindle afresh *ᵃ*the gift of God which is in you through *ᵃ*the laying on of my hands. **7** For God has not given us a *ᵃ*spirit of *¹*timidity, but of power and love and *²*discipline.

[Paul boasting about his suffering] 8 Therefore *ᵃ*do not be ashamed of the *ᵇ*testimony of our Lord or of me *ᶜ*His prisoner, but join with *me* in *ᵈ*suffering for the *ᵉ*gospel according to the power of God, **9** who has *ᵃ*saved us and *ᵇ*called us with a holy *ᶜ*calling, *ᵈ*not according to our works, but according to His own *ᵇ*purpose and grace which was granted us in *ᵉ*Christ Jesus from *ᶠ*all eternity, **10** but *ᵃ*now has been revealed by the *ᵇ*appearing of our Savior *ᶜ*Christ Jesus, who *ᵈ*abolished death and brought life and immortality to light through the gospel, **11** *ᵃ*for which I was appointed a preacher and an apostle and a teacher. **12** For this reason I also suffer these things, but *ᵃ*I am not ashamed; for I know *ᵇ*whom I have believed and I am convinced that He is able to *ᶜ*guard what I have entrusted to Him *¹*until *ᵈ*that day. **13** *¹ᵃ*Retain the *ᵇ*standard of *ᶜ*sound words *ᵈ*which you have heard from me, in the *ᵉ*faith and love which are in *ᶠ*Christ Jesus. **14** Guard, through the Holy Spirit who *ᵃ*dwells in us, the *¹ᵇ*treasure which has been entrusted to *you*.

[Paul is rejected] 15 You are aware of the fact that all who are in *¹ᵃ*Asia *ᵇ*turned away from me, among whom are Phygelus and Hermogenes. **16** The Lord grant mercy to *ᵃ*the house of Onesiphorus, for he often refreshed me and *ᵇ*was not ashamed of my *¹ᶜ*chains; **17** but when he was in Rome, he eagerly searched for me and found me — **18** the Lord grant to him to find mercy from the Lord on *ᵃ*that day — and you know very well what services he rendered at *ᵇ*Ephesus.

Discussion

In Paul's usual manner, he has to tell Timothy that he suffers for the gospel of Jesus Christ because he is such an ego centered individual.

Questioning the Passage

1. What does verse one mean?

The promise of life in Christ Jesus, as understood in Christian theology, encompasses several key aspects:

1. Salvation: Believers in Christ are promised salvation from sin and eternal separation from God. Through faith in Jesus Christ, individuals are forgiven of their sins and reconciled to God, securing eternal life with Him.

2. Redemption: The promise of life in Christ includes the redemption of humanity from the consequences of sin. Christ's sacrificial death on the cross is the ultimate act of redemption, offering liberation from bondage to sin and its effects.

3. Abundant life: Jesus promised abundant life to his followers (John 10:10). This abundant life is not just about material wealth or earthly success, but encompasses spiritual fulfillment, joy, peace, and purpose found in relationship with God.

4. Transformation: The promise of life in Christ involves transformation into the image of Christ. Through the work of the Holy Spirit, believers are progressively sanctified and empowered to live lives that reflect the character and teachings of Jesus.

5. Eternal life: One of the central promises of Christianity is eternal life, which is not just endless existence but life in communion with God. This eternal life begins at the moment of salvation and continues beyond physical death into eternity.

6. Hope: Life in Christ offers hope amid life's challenges and difficulties. Believers find hope in the promises of God's faithfulness, His presence with them, and the assurance of their ultimate victory in Christ.

Overall, the promise of life in Christ Jesus encompasses salvation, redemption, abundant life, transformation, eternal life, and hope, offering believers a profound sense of purpose, meaning, and fulfillment both in this life and in the life to come.

2. What is the difference between Jesus Christ and Christ Jesus?
    When Paul uses the term Jesus Christ, he is referring to the humanity of Jesus. When he uses the term Christ Jesus he is referring to the messianic purpose of Jesus Christ.

3. Why is Paul calling Timothy his beloved child? (v. 2)
    This is a term of endearment that a rabbi used for his disciples, especially the ones that were going to follow his way.

4. Does Paul ever call Yeshua "the Son?" (v. 2)
    The Apostle Paul did refer to Jesus as "the Son" in his letters. Paul's understanding of Jesus as the Son of God is central to his theology and is reflected in several passages:

1. Romans 1:3-4: In these verses, Paul writes about Jesus being "descended from David according to the flesh" and "designated Son of God in power according to the Spirit of holiness by his resurrection from the dead."

2. Galatians 4:4-6: Paul speaks of Jesus being "born of a woman, born under the law" and how God sent "his Son, born of a woman, born under the law, to redeem those who were under the law, so that we might receive adoption as sons."

3. Philippians 2:5-11: While not explicitly using the term "Son" here, Paul describes Jesus' humble obedience, even to the point of death on a cross, and how God highly exalted him and bestowed on him the name that is above every name.

4. Colossians 1:13-20: Paul speaks of Jesus as "the image of the invisible God, the firstborn of all creation" and describes his preeminence in all things, including creation itself, as well as his role in reconciling all things to God through his death on the cross.

These are just a few examples among many where Paul refers to Jesus as "the Son" or speaks about his divine nature and role in salvation. Paul's theology emphasizes Jesus' identity as the Son of God, who came to earth, lived among humanity, and ultimately provided redemption through his sacrificial death and resurrection.

5. What did Paul mean with "a clear conscience the way my forefathers did?" (v. 3) Paul said that he is trying to follow God in the same way that his ancestors did. He was not going to be swayed by the culture or the government. He was not going to allow the leadership at the Jerusalem Temple to stop him from fulfilling the mission that he was given.

6. Why was Timothy shedding tears? (v. 4)

    In this verse, the Apostle Paul expresses his deep affection for Timothy, recalling the tears that Timothy shed during their previous separation. Paul's longing to see Timothy again is evident, as he desires to be reunited with him and experience the joy that comes from being in his presence. This verse highlights the close relationship between Paul and Timothy and Paul's genuine care and concern for his young protégé in ministry.

7. Were timothy's mother and grandmother alive? (v. 5)

    According to Christian tradition, they were.

8. What is the gift of God? (v. 6)

    The gift from God is not explained by Paul in this verse. However, it could refer to the act of salvation and redemption from sin. It could refer to anything that God gives us as followers and believers in him. Paul also implies that following Yeshua will lead to more gifts.

9. Why does the gift of God need rekindling? (v. 6)

    At the time of the writing of this letter, things were not going well for the new Christians. There was pressure from all walks of life to force people out of the faith. Therefore, Paul reminded people they received the gift from God through Yeshua of salvation and that they should remember that the cultural pressures being put on them should not sway them from their faith.

10. Why does Paul insist one must suffer for the Gospel? (v. 8)

Paul is encouraging Timothy (and by extension, all believers) not to be ashamed of proclaiming the Gospel message or of Paul's own imprisonment for the sake of the Gospel.

Paul's insistence on suffering for the Gospel can be understood in several ways:

1. Identification with Christ: Paul often speaks of believers sharing in Christ's sufferings (Philippians 3:10), as Jesus himself suffered during his earthly ministry and particularly in his crucifixion. By enduring suffering for the sake of the Gospel, believers identify with Christ and take part in his redemptive work.

2. Testimony to the Gospel's Worth: Suffering for the Gospel serves as a testimony to its importance and worthiness. When believers endure trials and persecution for their faith, it shows the depth of their commitment to Christ and the truth of the Gospel message.

3. Growth and Maturity: Suffering can also lead to spiritual growth and maturity. Through trials, believers learn to rely more fully on God's strength and grace, developing perseverance, character, and hope (Romans 5:3-5).

4. Participation in God's Plan: Paul believed that suffering for the Gospel was part of God's sovereign plan for believers. In Colossians 1:24, he speaks of filling up "what is lacking in Christ's afflictions," suggesting that believers take part in the ongoing work of Christ through their own sufferings for the Gospel.

5. Reward and Glory: Despite the hardships of suffering for the Gospel, Paul often emphasizes the future reward and glory that await believers who remain faithful. In 2 Timothy 2:12, he writes, "if we endure, we will also reign with him."

Overall, Paul insists on suffering for the Gospel because he sees it as an integral aspect of the Christian life, one that leads to identification with Christ, testifies to the Gospel's worth, fosters growth and maturity, takes part in God's plan, and ultimately leads to reward and glory.

11. What does it mean to be saved? (v. 9)

To be saved is another synonym for the forgiveness of sin, redemption, atonement.

12. What is a holy calling? (v. 9)

A holy calling is one that is given from God to an individual.

13. What does it mean that we are granted grace in Christ Jesus before the ages? (v. 9)

Paul emphasizes several key theological points:

1. Salvation and Calling: Paul affirms that God has saved believers and called them to live a holy life. This calling involves not just salvation from sin but also a transformation in the way believers live, marked by righteousness and conformity to God's will.

2. God's Initiative: Paul underscores that this salvation and calling are not based on anything believers have done but are solely the result of God's initiative and

grace. It is not earned through good works or personal merit but is freely given by God out of His own purpose and grace.

3. Predestined Purpose: Paul suggests that God's grace and calling were given to believers in Christ Jesus before the beginning of time. This highlights the idea of predestination, suggesting that God had a predetermined plan for salvation and redemption through Jesus Christ.

Overall, 2 Timothy 1:9 emphasizes the sovereignty of God in salvation, the transformative nature of the Christian life, and the central role of grace in God's redemptive plan. It underscores the importance of living in light of God's calling and grace, recognizing that salvation is a gift from God based on His eternal purpose and not on human effort.

14. How did Yeshua abolish death? (v. 10)

Jewish people of Paul's day were struggling with the idea that death was the end of all existence. When the Greek invasion of the Near East occurred around 250 BCE, the Hellenistic idea of the separation of body and spirit was accepted. However, the idea was still considered somewhat new and Paul's day. There are Jewish people today that do not believe that there is any kind of afterlife. Yeshua was resurrection is considered the proof by Christianity that there is life after death. Therefore, Yeshua abolished death as being a finality, but a doorway into the next world.

15. What is the definition of a preacher, apostle, and teacher of the Gentiles? (v. 11)

In this verse, Paul is emphasizing his specific role and calling within the context of the Gospel. Here's a breakdown of its meaning:

1. "Of this gospel": Refers to the message of the Gospel, the good news about Jesus Christ, His death, resurrection, and the salvation offered through faith in Him.

2. "I was appointed": Indicates that Paul recognized his calling to his roles as a herald, apostle, and teacher within the framework of the Gospel. His appointment was not of his own accord but by divine calling.

3. "A herald": A herald is someone who proclaims or announces a message. Paul sees himself as appointed by God to proclaim the Gospel message to others, sharing it boldly and faithfully.

4. "An apostle": As an apostle, Paul was one of the chosen emissaries of Jesus Christ, commissioned to establish and oversee churches, spread the Gospel, and provide guidance and leadership to believers.

5. "A teacher": Paul also recognized his role as a teacher within the church. He was tasked with instructing believers in the truths of the Gospel, helping them grow in their understanding of God's Word and how to apply it to their lives.

Overall, in 2 Timothy 1:11, Paul is affirming his divine calling and the specific roles he has been given within the realm of the Gospel: to proclaim it as a herald, to establish and guide the church as an apostle, and to teach and instruct believers in its truths.

16. What is "that day" in verse twelve?

Paul believed Yeshua was going to return in his lifetime. The reference to that day is the day that Yeshua returns.

17. What is the treasure entrusted? (v. 14)

Paul considered his interpretation of Christianity to be a treasure that must be entrusted, secured, and never changed.

18. Who turned away from Paul in Asia? (v. 15)

Paul considered anyone that was not following his form of Christianity to be against him. He was especially critical of people who he taught his doctrine to and later on in life; they went with a different expression of Christianity.

19. What does it mean to "refresh?" (v. 16)

Paul is referring to when he visited the home that he was always welcome.

20. Why does the Lord need to grant mercy to the house of Onesiphorus? (v. 16)

Paul' was offering a blessing upon the family home because he was always welcome there.

21. What services did the house of Onesiphorus perform in Ephesus? (v. 18)

From verses sixteen through eighteen, it can be inferred that Onesiphorus showed kindness and care towards Paul during his time in Ephesus. He "refreshed" Paul, likely providing him with physical and emotional support, and he was not ashamed to associate himself with Paul even while Paul was imprisoned or facing hardships. When Onesiphorus later visited Rome, he made a concerted effort to locate Paul and offer him assistance. Overall, Onesiphorus's actions demonstrate his loyalty, compassion, and willingness to support Paul in his ministry, even at personal risk or inconvenience.

Biblical Personalities

1. Lois and Eunice

"There is only one mention of Lois and Eunice in the Bible. They were the grandmother and the mother of Paul's young protégé, <u>Timothy.</u> In Paul's second letter to Timothy, he mentions the faithfulness of these women in raising Timothy with such a devout faith. He writes, "I am reminded of your sincere faith, which first lived in your grandmother Lois and in your mother Eunice and, I am persuaded, now lives in you also" (2 Timothy 1:5).

Eunice was a Jewish believer who had been married to a Greek man (Acts 16:1), which would explain the fact that, as an infant, Timothy was not circumcised as all Jewish boys were. It was the responsibility of Jewish fathers to oversee that rite, and, since Timothy's father was Greek, circumcision would not have been his custom. Paul had Timothy circumcised before they began their missionary journeys together in order not to offend their Jewish audiences (verse 3).

Lois was Eunice's mother or her mother-in-law. She helped rear Timothy may indicate that Timothy's father had died or that the family all lived together, which was not uncommon in those days. It is possible that the father had died while Timothy was young, since Paul takes on a fatherly role with Timothy and often refers to him as "my true son in the faith" (1 Corinthians 4:17; 1 Timothy 1:2, 18).

Timothy's godly upbringing is referenced again in 2 Timothy 3:14–15: "You, however, continue in the things you have learned and become convinced of, knowing from whom you have learned them, and that from childhood you have known the sacred writings which are able to give you the wisdom that leads to salvation through faith which is in Christ Jesus." Paul's mention of those "from whom you have learned" probably refers to Timothy's godly mother and grandmother, Eunice and Lois, who taught him the Jewish Scriptures from infancy. They, along with Timothy, received Paul's teaching about the Messiah and continued to train young Timothy in the things of Christ.

Lois and Eunice are examples of the powerful influence a mother or grandmother can have on a young man's life. Many personal testimonies include statements such as "My mom (or grandma) took me to church, taught me right, and prayed for me every day." Paul recognized the life-changing contributions of these two women in a day when women were rarely mentioned by name. He honored their impact in preparing his young protégé, who later joined Paul in his travels (Romans 16:21) and eventually became the pastor of the church at Ephesus (1 Timothy 1:3). Lois and Eunice should encourage all Christian mothers and grandmothers, reminding them that their godly influence has an eternal impact on the lives and futures of their children and grandchildren."[4]

2. Phygelus

"One of the Christians who deserted Paul at the time of his 2nd imprisonment at Rome. Paul mentions him, along with Hermogenes, as being among those "that are in Asia," who turned away from him then. What is meant may be that Phygelus and Hermogenes, along with other native Christians from proconsular Asia, were in Rome when he was brought before the emperor's tribunal the second time, and

---

[4] 1. GotQuestions.org, "Home," GotQuestions.org, May 11, 2017, https://www.gotquestions.org/Lois-and-Eunice.html.

that they had not merely taken no measures to stand by and support him, but that they had deserted him.

The meaning, however, may be that the turning away of Phygelus and Hermogenes from Paul occurred, not in Rome, but in Asia itself.

The times during and immediately following the Neronic persecution were more dreadful than can easily be conceived, and the temptation was strong to forsake the Christian name, and to do so in a wholesale fashion. A great community like the Christian church in Ephesus or in Rome felt the terrible pressure of those times, when for a mere word-a word, however, denying the Lord who bought them-men were immediately set free from persecution, from the loss of property or of home, and from death. 1 Peter records how the aftermath of the Neronic persecution had extended far indeed from Rome, where it had originated. Peter asks the Christians not to give way under "the fiery trial" which is trying them (1 Peter 4:12), and those whom he thus addresses were the members of the church throughout Pontus, Galatia, Cappadocia, Asia and Bithynia (1 Peter 1:1). The epistles to the seven churches in Asia in the Apocalypse also show how sorely persecution had raged throughout that province."[5]

3. Hermogenes

Hermogenes was a Christian, mentioned by Paul as having, along with Phygellus and "all that are in Asia," turned away from him. It is not clear when or where the defection of those Asiatic Christians from the apostle took place, whether it was at Rome at the time of Paul's second imprisonment there, and especially on the occasion of his being brought before the emperor's supreme court, to be tried on

---

[5] 1. Topical bible: Phygellus, accessed February 11, 2024, https://biblehub.com/topical/p/phygellus.htm.

a charge now involving the death penalty, or whether it was at some previous time in Ephesus."[6]

4. Oneseiphorus

"(Greek: Ονησιφόρος; meaning "bringing profit" or "useful") was a Christian referred to in the New Testament letter of Second Timothy (2 Tim 1:16–18 and 2 Tim 4:19). According to the letter sent by St. Paul, Onesiphorus sought out Paul who was imprisoned at the time in Rome."[7]

Culture Section

Questioning the passage

1. What does "the laying on of my hands" mean? (v. 6)

This expression refers to ordination. This is an ancient Near East custom where a rabbi was ordained by his teacher to go out and preach. When sincere friends converse with one another, they place a hand on each other's shoulders. The placing of both hands on the shoulders became part of the ordination ritual. The laying of hands on a person is an act of consecration, the person is being called out to do the work of the Lord.[8]

Thoughts

Paul entrusted Timothy with taking the gospel into Ephesus and reminding the people of it. Today, many people who call themselves Christians have forgotten what it means to be a Christian. Church attendance is pathetically low, and churches are not evangelizing like they used to that one day the message of the gospel will be lost. It is difficult to go out and preach the gospel of Jesus Christ in the current world. However,

[6] 1. Topical bible: Hermogenes, accessed February 11, 2024, https://biblehub.com/topical/h/hermogenes.htm.
[7] 1. "Onesiphorus," Wikipedia, January 31, 2024, https://en.wikipedia.org/wiki/Onesiphorus.
[8] 1. Rocco A. Errico and George M. Lamsa, *Aramaic Light on Galatians through Hebrews: A Commentary Based on Aramaic, the Language of Jesus, and Ancient near Eastern Customs* (Smyma, GA: Noohra Foundation, 2005).

people need to learn to do it and start doing it before it is too late. There is also the problem in the world that there are numerous expressions of Christianity that it has now hard to tell which one is correct. What is worse is when different denominations say that they are the only true expression. This practice needs to stop, and it needs to stop now.

Chapter Two

Language

Peshitta	New American Standard 1995
2Timothy 2:1 Thou therefore, my son, be strong in the grace which is by Jesus the Messiah. **2** And the things thou hast heard from me by many witnesses, these commit thou to faithful men, who are competent to teach others also. **3** And endure evils, as a good soldier of Jesus the Messiah. **4** No man, on becoming a soldier, entangleth himself with the business of the world; that he may please him who enlisted him. **5** And if one contend [in the games], he is not crowned, unless he contendeth according to the rules. **6** The husbandman who laboreth, ought first to feed on his fruits. **7** Consider what I say. Our Lord give thee wisdom in all things. **8** Be mindful of Jesus the Messiah, that he arose from the dead; who was of the seed of David, according to my gospel, **9** in which I suffer evils unto bonds, as if an evil-doer: but the word of God is not in bonds. **10** Therefore I endure every thing, for the elect's sake; that they also may obtain life, in Jesus the Messiah, with eternal glory. **11** Faithful is the saying, For if we shall have died with him, we shall also live with him; **12** and, if we shall have suffered, we shall also reign with him. But if we shall have rejected him, he will reject us. **13** And if we shall have not believed in him, he abideth in his fidelity; for he cannot reject himself. **14** Of these things admonish thou them and charge [them,] before our Lord, that they dispute not, with unprofitable words,	**2Timothy 2:1** You therefore, my [1][a]son, [b]be strong in the grace that is in [c]Christ Jesus. **2** The things [a]which you have heard from me in the presence of [b]many witnesses, [c]entrust these to [d]faithful men who will be [e]able to teach others also. **3** [a]Suffer hardship with *me,* as a good [b]soldier of [c]Christ Jesus. **4** No soldier in active service [a]entangles himself in the affairs of everyday life, so that he may please the one who enlisted him as a soldier. **5** Also if anyone [a]competes as an athlete, he [1]does not win the prize unless he competes according to the rules. **6** [a]The hard-working farmer ought to be the first to receive his share of the crops. **7** Consider what I say, for the Lord will give you understanding in everything. **2Timothy 2:8** Remember Jesus Christ, [a]risen from the dead, [b]descendant of David, [c]according to my gospel, **9** [1]for which I [a]suffer hardship even to [b]imprisonment as a [c]criminal; but [d]the word of God [e]is not imprisoned. **10** For this reason [a]I endure all things for [b]the sake of those who are chosen, [c]so that they also may obtain the [d]salvation which is in [e]Christ Jesus *and* with *it*[f]eternal glory. **11** [a]It is a trustworthy statement: For [b]if we died with Him, we will also live with Him;

to the subversion of those who hear them. **15** And study to present thyself before God, perfectly, a laborer who is not ashamed, one who correctly announceth the word of truth. **16** Avoid vain discourses, in which there is no profit; for they very much add to the wickedness of those occupied with them. **17** And their discourse, like an eating cancer, will lay hold upon many. And one of these is Hymeneus, and another Philetus; **18** who have wandered from the truth, while they say, The resurrection of the dead hath passed: and they subvert the faith of some. **19** But the firm foundation of God standeth; and it hath this seal, The Lord knoweth them who are his: and, Let every one who invoketh the name of our Lord, stand aloof from iniquity. **20** But in a great house, there are not only vessels of gold or silver, but also of wood and of pottery; and some of them for honor, and some for dishonor. **21** If therefore any one purge himself from these things, he will be a pure vessel for honor, fit for the use of his Lord, and prepared for every good work. **22** Fly from all the lusts of youth; and follow after righteousness, and faith, and love, and peace, with them that invoke our Lord with a pure heart. **23** Avoid those foolish discussions which afford no instruction; for thou knowest, that they generate contests. **24** And a servant of our Lord ought not to contend, but to be mild towards every one, and instructive, and patient; **25** that with mildness he may enlighten those who dispute against him, if perhaps God may give them repentance, and they may acknowledge the truth, **26** and may recollect themselves, and may

12 If we endure, *a*we will also reign with Him;

If we *1b*deny Him, He also will deny us;

13 If we are faithless, *a*He remains faithful, for *b*He cannot deny Himself.

2Timothy 2:14 Remind *them* of these things, and solemnly *a*charge *them* in the presence of God not to *b*wrangle about words, which is useless *and leads* to the ruin of the hearers. **15** Be diligent to *a*present yourself approved to God as a workman who does not need to be ashamed, accurately handling *b*the word of truth. **16** But *a*avoid *b*worldly *and* empty chatter, for *1*it will lead to further ungodliness, **17** and their *1*talk will spread like *2*gangrene. Among them are *a*Hymenaeus and Philetus, **18** *men* who have gone astray from the truth saying that *a*the resurrection has already taken place, and they upset *b*the faith of some. **19** Nevertheless, the *a*firm foundation of God stands, having this *b*seal, "*c*The Lord knows those who are His," and, "*d*Everyone who names the name of the Lord is to abstain from wickedness."

2Timothy 2:20 Now in a large house there are not only gold and silver vessels, but also vessels of wood and of earthenware, and *a*some to honor and some to dishonor. **21** Therefore, if anyone cleanses himself from *a*these *things,* he will be a vessel for honor, sanctified, useful to the Master, *b*prepared for every good work. **22** Now *a*flee from youthful lusts and pursue righteousness, *b*faith, love *and* peace, with those who *c*call on the Lord *d*from a pure heart. **23** But refuse foolish

escape out of the snare of Satan, at whose pleasure they have been held ensnared.	and ignorant [a]speculations, knowing that they [b]produce [1]quarrels. **24** [a]The Lord's bond-servant must not be quarrelsome, but be kind to all, [b]able to teach, patient when wronged, **25** [a]with gentleness correcting those who are in opposition, [b]if perhaps God may grant them repentance leading to [c]the knowledge of the truth, **26** and they may come to their senses *and escape* from [a]the snare of the devil, having been [b]held captive [1]by him to do his will.

2Timothy 2:1
[1]Or *child*
[a]2 Tim 1:2
[b]Eph 6:10
[c]2 Tim 1:1

2Timothy 2:2
[a]2 Tim 1:13
[b]1 Tim 6:12
[c]1 Tim 1:18
[d]1 Tim 1:12
[e]2 Cor 2:14ff; 3:5

2Timothy 2:3
[a]2 Tim 1:8
[b]1 Cor 9:7; 1 Tim 1:18
[c]2 Tim 1:1

2Timothy 2:4
[a]2 Pet 2:20

2Timothy 2:5
[1]Lit *is not crowned*
[a]1 Cor 9:25

2Timothy 2:6
[a]1 Cor 9:10

2Timothy 2:8
[a]Acts 2:24
[b]Matt 1:1
[c]Rom 2:16

2Timothy 2:9

[1]Lit *in which*
[a]2 Tim 1:8; 2:3
[b]Phil 1:7
[c]Luke 23:32
[d]1 Thess 1:8
[e]Acts 28:31; 2 Tim 4:17

2Timothy 2:10

[a]Col 1:24
[b]Luke 18:7; Titus 1:1
[c]2 Cor 1:6; 1 Thess 5:9
[d]1 Cor 1:21
[e]2 Tim 1:1; 2:1, 3
[f]2 Cor 4:17; 1 Pet 5:10

2Timothy 2:11

[a]1 Tim 1:15
[b]Rom 6:8; 1 Thess 5:10

2Timothy 2:12

[1]Lit *will deny*
[a]Matt 19:28; Luke 22:29; Rom 5:17; 8:17
[b]Matt 10:33; Luke 12:9; 1 Tim 5:8

2Timothy 2:13

[a]Rom 3:3; 1 Cor 1:9
[b]Num 23:19; Titus 1:2

2Timothy 2:14

[a]1 Tim 5:21; 2 Tim 4:1
[b]1 Tim 6:4; 2 Tim 2:23; Titus 3:9

2Timothy 2:15

[a]Rom 6:13; James 1:12
[b]Eph 1:13; James 1:18

2Timothy 2:16

[1]Lit *they will make further progress in ungodliness*
[a]Titus 3:9
[b]1 Tim 1:9; 6:20

2Timothy 2:17

[1]Lit *word*
[2]Or *cancer*
[a]1 Tim 1:20

2Timothy 2:18

[a]1 Cor 15:12
[b]1 Tim 1:19; Titus 1:11

2Timothy 2:19

[a]Is 28:16f; 1 Tim 3:15
[b]John 3:33
[c]John 10:14; 1 Cor 8:3
[d]Luke 13:27; 1 Cor 1:2

2Timothy 2:20

[a]Rom 9:21

2Timothy 2:21

[a]1 Tim 6:11; 2 Tim 2:16-18
[b]2 Cor 9:8; Eph 2:10; 2 Tim 3:17

2Timothy 2:22

[a]1 Tim 6:11
[b]1 Tim 1:14

^cActs 7:59
^d1 Tim 1:5

2Timothy 2:23

¹Lit *fightings*
^a1 Tim 6:4; 2 Tim 2:14; Titus 3:9
^bTitus 3:9; James 4:1

2Timothy 2:24

^a1 Tim 3:3; Titus 1:7
^b1 Tim 3:2

2Timothy 2:25

^aGal 6:1; Titus 3:2; 1 Pet 3:15
^bActs 8:22
^c1 Tim 2:4

2Timothy 2:26

¹Or *by him, to do His will*
^a1 Tim 3:7
^bLuke 5:10

2Timothy 2:1   Σὺ οὖν, τέκνον μου, ἐνδυναμοῦ ἐν τῇ χάριτι τῇ ἐν χριστῷ Ἰησοῦ. **2** Καὶ ἃ ἤκουσας παρ' ἐμοῦ διὰ πολλῶν μαρτύρων, ταῦτα παράθου πιστοῖς ἀνθρώποις, οἵτινες ἱκανοὶ ἔσονται καὶ ἑτέρους διδάξαι. **3** Σὺ οὖν κακοπάθησον ὡς καλὸς στρατιώτης Ἰησοῦ χριστοῦ. **4** Οὐδεὶς στρατευόμενος ἐμπλέκεται ταῖς τοῦ βίου πραγματείαις, ἵνα τῷ στρατολογήσαντι ἀρέσῃ. **5** Ἐὰν δὲ καὶ ἀθλῇ τις, οὐ στεφανοῦται ἐὰν μὴ νομίμως ἀθλήσῃ. **6** Τὸν κοπιῶντα γεωργὸν δεῖ πρῶτον τῶν καρπῶν μεταλαμβάνειν. **7** Νόει ἃ λέγω· δώῃ γὰρ σοι ὁ κύριος σύνεσιν ἐν πᾶσιν. **8** Μνημόνευε Ἰησοῦν χριστὸν ἐγηγερμένον ἐκ νεκρῶν, ἐκ σπέρματος Δαυίδ, κατὰ τὸ εὐαγγέλιόν μου· **9** ἐν ᾧ κακοπαθῶ μέχρι δεσμῶν, ὡς κακοῦργος· ἀλλ' ὁ λόγος τοῦ θεοῦ οὐ δέδεται. **10** Διὰ τοῦτο πάντα ὑπομένω διὰ τοὺς ἐκλεκτούς, ἵνα καὶ αὐτοὶ σωτηρίας τύχωσιν τῆς ἐν χριστῷ Ἰησοῦ, μετὰ δόξης αἰωνίου. **11** Πιστὸς ὁ λόγος· εἰ γὰρ συναπεθάνομεν, καὶ συζήσομεν· **12** εἰ ὑπομένομεν, καὶ συμβασιλεύσομεν· εἰ ἀρνούμεθα, κἀκεῖνος ἀρνήσεται ἡμᾶς· **13** εἰ ἀπιστοῦμεν, ἐκεῖνος πιστὸς μένει· ἀρνήσασθαι ἑαυτὸν οὐ δύναται.

2Timothy 2:14   Ταῦτα ὑπομίμνησκε, διαμαρτυρόμενος ἐνώπιον τοῦ κυρίου μὴ λογομαχεῖν εἰς οὐδὲν χρήσιμον, ἐπὶ καταστροφῇ τῶν ἀκουόντων. **15** Σπούδασον σεαυτὸν δόκιμον παραστῆσαι τῷ θεῷ, ἐργάτην ἀνεπαίσχυντον, ὀρθοτομοῦντα τὸν λόγον τῆς ἀληθείας. **16** Τὰς δὲ βεβήλους κενοφωνίας περιΐστασο· ἐπὶ πλεῖον γὰρ προκόψουσιν ἀσεβείας, **17** καὶ ὁ λόγος αὐτῶν ὡς γάγγραινα νομὴν ἕξει· ὧν ἐστιν Ὑμέναιος καὶ Φιλητός· **18** οἵτινες περὶ τὴν ἀλήθειαν ἠστόχησαν, λέγοντες τὴν ἀνάστασιν ἤδη γεγονέναι, καὶ ἀνατρέπουσιν τὴν τινων πίστιν. **19** Ὁ μέντοι στερεὸς θεμέλιος τοῦ θεοῦ ἕστηκεν, ἔχων τὴν σφραγῖδα ταύτην, Ἔγνω κύριος τοὺς ὄντας αὐτοῦ, καὶ, Ἀποστήτω ἀπὸ ἀδικίας πᾶς ὁ ὀνομάζων τὸ ὄνομα κυρίου. **20** Ἐν μεγάλῃ δὲ οἰκίᾳ οὐκ ἔστιν μόνον σκεύη χρυσᾶ καὶ ἀργυρᾶ, ἀλλὰ καὶ ξύλινα καὶ ὀστράκινα, καὶ ἃ μὲν εἰς τιμήν, ἃ δὲ εἰς ἀτιμίαν. **21** Ἐὰν οὖν τις ἐκκαθάρῃ ἑαυτὸν ἀπὸ τούτων, ἔσται σκεῦος εἰς τιμήν, ἡγιασμένον, καὶ εὔχρηστον τῷ δεσπότῃ, εἰς πᾶν ἔργον ἀγαθὸν ἡτοιμασμένον. **22** Τὰς δὲ νεωτερικὰς ἐπιθυμίας φεῦγε· δίωκε δὲ δικαιοσύνην, πίστιν, ἀγάπην, εἰρήνην, μετὰ τῶν ἐπικαλουμένων τὸν κύριον ἐκ καθαρᾶς καρδίας. **23** Τὰς δὲ μωρὰς καὶ ἀπαιδεύτους ζητήσεις παραιτοῦ, εἰδὼς ὅτι γεννῶσιν μάχας. **24** Δοῦλον δὲ κυρίου οὐ δεῖ μάχεσθαι, ἀλλ' ἤπιον εἶναι πρὸς πάντας, διδακτικόν, ἀνεξίκακον, **25** ἐν πραότητι παιδεύοντα τοὺς ἀντιδιατιθεμένους· μήποτε δῷ αὐτοῖς ὁ θεὸς μετάνοιαν εἰς ἐπίγνωσιν ἀληθείας, **26** καὶ ἀνανήψωσιν ἐκ τῆς τοῦ διαβόλου παγίδος, ἐζωγρημένοι ὑπ' αὐτοῦ εἰς τὸ ἐκείνου θέλημα.

Language
  Process of Discovery

   Linguistics Section

   Linguistic Structure

[Be strong] **1** You therefore, my [1][a]son, [b]be strong in the grace that is in [c]Christ Jesus. **2** The things [a]which you have heard from me in the presence of [b]many witnesses, [c]entrust these to [d]faithful men who will be [e]able to teach others also. **3** [a]Suffer hardship with *me,* as a good [b]soldier of [c]Christ Jesus. **4** No soldier in active service [a]entangles himself in the affairs of everyday life, so that he may please the one who enlisted him as a soldier. **5** Also if anyone [a]competes as an athlete, he [1]does not win the prize unless he competes according to the rules. **6** [a]The hard-working farmer ought to be the first to receive his share of the crops. **7** Consider what I say, for the Lord will give you understanding in everything.

[Continued] **8** Remember Jesus Christ, [a]risen from the dead, [b]descendant of David, [c]according to my gospel, **9** [1]for which I [a]suffer hardship even to [b]imprisonment as a [c]criminal; but [d]the word of God [e]is not imprisoned. **10** For this reason [a]I endure all things for [b]the sake of those who are chosen, [c]so that they also may obtain the [d]salvation which is in [e]Christ Jesus *and* with *it* [f]eternal glory. **11** [a]It is a trustworthy statement:

    For [b]if we died with Him, we will also live with Him;

12   If we endure, [a]we will also reign with Him;

    If we [1][b]deny Him, He also will deny us;

13   If we are faithless, [a]He remains faithful, for [b]He cannot deny Himself.

[Do not let outsiders sway Paul's believers] **14** Remind *them* of these things, and solemnly [a]charge *them* in the presence of God not to [b]wrangle about words, which is useless *and leads* to the ruin of the hearers. **15** Be diligent to [a]present yourself approved to God as a workman who does not need to be ashamed, accurately handling [b]the word of truth. **16** But [a]avoid [b]worldly *and* empty chatter, for [1]it will lead to further ungodliness, **17** and their [1]talk will spread like [2]gangrene. Among them are [a]Hymenaeus and Philetus, **18** *men* who have gone astray from the truth saying that [a]the resurrection has already taken place, and they upset [b]the faith of some. **19** Nevertheless, the [a]firm foundation of God stands, having this [b]seal, "[c]The Lord knows those who are His," and, "[d]Everyone who names the name of the Lord is to abstain from wickedness."

[Continued] **20** Now in a large house there are not only gold and silver vessels, but also vessels of wood and of earthenware, and [a]some to honor and some to dishonor. **21** Therefore, if anyone cleanses himself from [a]these *things,* he will be a vessel for honor, sanctified, useful to the Master, *prepared for every good work. **22** Now *flee from youthful lusts and pursue righteousness, *faith, love *and* peace, with those who *call on the Lord *from a pure heart. **23** But refuse foolish and ignorant *speculations, knowing that they *produce ¹quarrels. **24** *The Lord's bond-servant must not be quarrelsome, but be kind to all, *able to teach, patient when wronged, **25** *with gentleness correcting those who are in opposition, *if perhaps God may grant them repentance leading to *the knowledge of the truth, **26** and they may come to their senses *and escape* from *the snare of the devil, having been *held captive ¹by him to do his will.

Discussion

This chapter is a continuation of Paul's concern that Timothy and the converts in Asia Minor must stay loyal to his teachings.

Questioning the Passage

1. What is the grace in Christ Jesus? (v. 1)

   The "grace in Christ Jesus" refers to the unmerited favor and divine assistance extended to humanity through the person and work of Jesus Christ. In Christian theology, grace is understood as God's freely given love, forgiveness, and salvation, which people do not earn through their own efforts but receive as a gift through faith in Jesus Christ.

   The concept of grace in Christianity is central to the belief in salvation. It emphasizes that salvation is not something that can be achieved through human works or efforts, but it is received solely by God's grace through faith. This grace is often associated with God's love and mercy, demonstrated supremely in the sacrificial death of Jesus Christ on the cross for the redemption of humanity's sins.

In the New Testament of the Bible, the apostle Paul frequently writes about the concept of grace, emphasizing that believers are saved by grace through faith and not by their own works (Ephesians 2:8-9). This grace is described as abundant (Romans 5:17), sufficient (2 Corinthians 12:9), and transformative (Titus 2:11-12).

Overall, the "grace in Christ Jesus" represents the foundational belief in Christianity that salvation and reconciliation with God are made possible through the undeserved favor and love of God, made manifest through Jesus Christ.

2. Who were the witnesses Paul sent in verse two?

Paul is referring to the men and women who were with him when he instructed Timothy.

3. How does the soldier metaphor apply to the Gospel? (v. 3)

In 2 Timothy 2, the soldier metaphor is used by the apostle Paul to illustrate several aspects of Christian discipleship and endurance in the face of adversity. Let's break down how this metaphor works in the context of the passage:

1. Endurance: Paul encourages Timothy to "be strong in the grace that is in Christ Jesus" (2 Timothy 2:1). Just as a soldier must endure hardship and stay strong in the face of challenges, so too must Christians remain steadfast in their faith, relying on the grace and strength that come from their relationship with Christ.

2. Single-mindedness: Paul urges Timothy to "no soldier gets entangled in civilian pursuits, since his aim is to please the one who enlisted him" (2 Timothy 2:4).

This highlights the importance of maintaining focus and not allowing oneself to be distracted by worldly concerns or entanglements. Instead, Christians are called to prioritize their commitment to Christ and strive to live in a manner that pleases Him.

3. Hard Work and Discipline: The soldier metaphor also emphasizes the importance of diligence and discipline in the Christian life. Paul likens the Christian walk to that of an athlete who competes according to the rules (2 Timothy 2:5), implying that just as athletes must train and exert effort to succeed, so too must Christians be diligent in their spiritual growth and service.

4. Suffering and Endurance: Paul acknowledges that serving Christ may involve suffering and hardship, comparing it to enduring as a good soldier (2 Timothy 2:3). However, he encourages Timothy to endure, reminding him that those who endure will also reign with Christ (2 Timothy 2:12).

Overall, the soldier metaphor in 2 Timothy 2 serves to underscore the challenges and responsibilities of the Christian life, while also offering encouragement and exhortation to remain steadfast in faith, disciplined in conduct, and focused on the ultimate goal of pleasing Christ.

4. What are everyday affairs of life? (v. 4)
The every day for affairs of life would be referring to mealtime and other hygiene activities. The daily activities that one must perform to stay alive must not take priority over the preaching of the gospel of Jesus Christ.

5. What are the rules of the Gospel? (v. 5)

This verse employs the metaphor of an athlete to convey a spiritual truth. While it doesn't directly list "rules of the gospel," it does convey the importance of adhering to certain principles or standards in the Christian life. Here's how we can understand it:

1. Discipline and Diligence: Just as an athlete must train rigorously and follow the rules of their sport to win a prize, so too must Christians discipline themselves and adhere to the principles of the gospel to receive the reward of eternal life.

2. Obedience to God's Word: The "rules" referred to here likely encompass the teachings and commandments of Jesus Christ as found in the gospel. Christians are called to live according to the standards set forth by Christ, which include love, righteousness, humility, and obedience to God's Word.

3. Faithfulness and Perseverance: Like athletes who must persevere through challenges and hardships to achieve victory, Christians are called to remain faithful and steadfast in their commitment to Christ, even in the face of trials and temptations.

Overall, while 2 Timothy 2:5 doesn't provide an explicit list of rules, it underscores the importance of living according to the principles and teachings of the gospel in order to receive the ultimate prize of eternal life with Christ.

6. What does verse six mean?

This verse utilizes the metaphor of a farmer to convey a spiritual lesson. Here's an interpretation of what this metaphor signifies:

1. Persistence and Diligence: Just as a farmer works hard and diligently tends to his crops, so too should Christians persistently labor in their spiritual endeavors. This includes faithful prayer, studying the Scriptures, serving others, and living out the teachings of Christ.

2. Expectation of Reward: The farmer expects to receive a share of the crops as a reward for his labor. Similarly, Christians can expect spiritual blessings and rewards for their faithful service and obedience to God.

3. First to Receive: The phrase "the first to receive" suggests that there is a reward awaiting those who labor faithfully. In the context of Christian discipleship, this may imply receiving spiritual blessings, growth in faith, and ultimately, the promise of eternal life with God.

Overall, the farmer reference in 2 Timothy 2:6 encourages believers to be diligent, persistent, and expectant of the rewards that come from faithfully serving and obeying God in their spiritual journey.

7. Why does Paul add "descendant of David" if Timothy has been taught these things? (v. 8)

"Within the context of calling for Timothy's loyalty to Paul and the gospel, Paul defines that gospel: it is the account of Jesus the Messiah as the fulfillment of prophecy; it is also the account of Christ, raised from the dead. Perhaps ἐκ σπέρματος Δαυίδ, "from [the] seed of David," is the idea that just as Jesus Christ suffered and persevered, so also Timothy should willingly suffer and persevere."[9]

8. What is Paul's gospel? (v. 8)

Paul had decided what the gospel of Yeshua was all about. When he refers to his gospel, he is saying his interpretation of what the life and death of Yeshua was about.

9. Who is the elect (chosen)? (v. 10)

The elect is a concept that has various meanings. In its pure meaning, it is that there is a group of people that are selected to go to heaven. In Paul's day, it would be anyone who follows his form of Christianity. Later in the Middle Ages it becomes known as a group of people who were pre-selected by God to go to heaven no matter what they did in life.

10. Who created the trustworthy statement from verses eleven through thirteen?

If Paul is not the author, it is unknown who is.

"Salvation from hell is a free gift received through faith alone in the Lord Jesus Christ. The regenerate person is secure in his possession of eternal life from the moment of saving faith because of the faithfulness of God to him. In stark contrast, true, vibrant discipleship involves a costly commitment of a believer's life, expressed through steadfast obedience to Jesus Christ.[ ] The enduring

<hr>

[9] Mounce, W. D. (2000). *Pastoral Epistles* (Vol. 46, p. 511). Word, Incorporated.

disciple is promised special reward in Christ's future kingdom because of his faithfulness to God.

These fundamental truths are proclaimed by the Apostle Paul in **2 Tim 2:11-13**. This passage revolves around four problematic conditional clauses (if…[then] constructions). In these verses Paul maintains that a believer in Christ is secure in his ownership of eternal life, yet his Christian life will be scrutinized by the Lord and special privilege and reward will be conferred on him only if he is found to have been faithful."[10]

11. What resurrection is referred to in verse eighteen? (v. 18)

This verse is one where Paul addresses the heresy of the time that the resurrection has already occurred. Here, their resurrection refers to a spiritual awakening. It is also a reference that a person will never die because they were followers of Yeshua. It is one of the few times that Paul tells us what the heresy is that he has fighting against.

12. What is the firm foundation of God? (v. 19)

In this verse, the "firm foundation of God" refers to the unwavering truth and security found in God and His promises. Here's a breakdown of what this means:

1. Security in God's Truth: The solid foundation of God represents the unchanging truth and reliability of God's character, His Word, and His promises. This foundation provides security and stability for believers amidst the uncertainties and challenges of life.

---

[10] 1. GES Webmaster, "Secure yet Scrutinized – 2 Timothy 2:11-13," Grace Evangelical Society, September 1, 1988, https://faithalone.org/journal-articles/secure-yet-scrutinized-2-timothy-211-13/.

2. Inscription of Ownership: The verse mentions an inscription on this firm foundation: "The Lord knows those who are his." This highlights the intimate relationship between God and His people. God intimately knows and cares for those who belong to Him, providing reassurance and comfort to believers.

3. Call to Holiness: The verse also emphasizes the importance of holy living for those who claim to belong to the Lord. It states, "Everyone who confesses the name of the Lord must turn away from wickedness." This underscores the necessity for believers to live lives that are aligned with God's will and characterized by righteousness and obedience.

Overall, 2 Timothy 2:19 affirms the unshakeable nature of God's truth and the security found in belonging to Him. It encourages believers to remain faithful, knowing that they are firmly established on the solid foundation of God's love, grace, and truth.

13. What does it mean to be sanctified? (v. 21)

    To be sanctified means to set oneself aside for the work of the Lord.

14. What are good works? (v. 21)

    Christian good works typically refer to acts of kindness, compassion, charity, and service that are inspired by Christian beliefs and values. These actions are a way for Christians to express their faith and show their love for God and their fellow human beings. While specific practices may vary among different Christian denominations and individual believers, some common examples of Christian good works include:

1. Charity and generosity: Christians are often encouraged to help those in need by giving to the poor, feeding the hungry, clothing the naked, and providing shelter to the homeless. This can involve volunteering at soup kitchens, donating to charitable organizations, or participating in mission trips to impoverished areas.

2. Acts of kindness and compassion: Christians are called to show love and compassion to others, including strangers, neighbors, and even enemies. This can involve offering a listening ear, providing emotional support, or offering practical assistance to those who are struggling or suffering.

3. Social justice and advocacy: Many Christians believe in working to address systemic injustices and advocate for the rights and dignity of all people, particularly the marginalized and oppressed. This can involve speaking out against discrimination, working to end poverty and inequality, and advocating for policies that promote justice and human rights.

4. Mission and evangelism: Some Christians engage in activities aimed at sharing their faith with others and bringing more people into the Christian community. This can involve evangelistic outreach, missionary work, and sharing the message of Jesus Christ through words and actions.

5. Prayer and spiritual support: Christians believe in the power of prayer to bring about positive change in the world and to provide comfort and support to those in need. Christians may pray for individuals facing challenges, for communities affected by tragedy or disaster, and for the well-being of the world as a whole.

Overall, Christian good works are motivated by a desire to follow the example of Jesus Christ, who taught his followers to love one another, serve others selflessly, and work for the kingdom of God. These acts of service and compassion are seen as expressions of faith and obedience to God's commandments to love God and love one's neighbor as oneself.

15. What are youthful lusts/passions? (v. 22)

The "evil desires of youth" or "youthful lusts" refer to the temptations and impulses that are often associated with young age. These could include various forms of sensual or selfish desires, such as positing physical pleasure, materialism, pride, and reckless behavior.

The verse is advising Timothy, a young leader in the early Christian church, to avoid being swayed by these temptations and instead to focus on qualities and virtues that are aligned with Christian values. It encourages him to pursue righteousness, faith, love, and peace, along with fellow believers who are devoted to serving God sincerely.

So, "fleeing youthful lusts" essentially means avoiding or turning away from the negative influences and behaviors that are common in youth culture, and instead, dedicating oneself to a life of spiritual growth, moral integrity, and service to others.

16. What was a bond-servant? (v. 24)

A bondservant in this verse is a person who works only for Yeshua.

17. What does it mean that God may grant repentance? (v. 25)

Paul had a difficult time in the letters between the theological position of Yeshua's granting of repentance and God's granting of repentance. It matters who his audience was at the time. Jews believe only God can grant forgiveness, which is obtained through repentance. The Mithras converted churches believe Yeshua is the only one that can offer this.

Biblical Personalities

1. Hymenaeus

A heretical teacher at Ephesus, an opponent of Paul, mentioned with Alexander in 1 Timothy 1:20 and with Philetus in 2 Timothy 2:17. The same man is doubtless in view in both passages. That he is mentioned first in both places implies that he was the leader among these false teachers.

Hymenaeus and Alexander were among those who, rejecting conscience, had made shipwreck of their faith (1 Tim 1:20). Paul's delivery of them to Satan has been much discussed (cf. 1 Cor 5:5). Some take the meaning to be simply excommunication from the church, thereby placing them back into the world, the sphere of Satan. Others think it rather signifies supernaturally inflicted bodily punishment. A combination of both views may be involved. That more than mere excommunication is meant seems clear (Job 2:6, 7; 1 Cor 11:30; Rev 2:22) when compared with the cases of apostolic discipline in Acts 5:1-11; 13:11. The discipline, whatever its precise nature, was remedial in its intention, "that they may learn not to blaspheme," i.e. that they may cease their railing against the true Gospel.

The discipline had not produced the desired repentance in Hymenaeus when 2 Timothy 2:17, 18 was written. The doctrinal error of Hymenaeus and Philetus, destructively spreading like gangrene, was their denial of an eschatological resurrection. They allegorized the resurrection by insisting that it was a past spiritual experience, having occurred when they were raised from ignorance and sin as they came to know the true God. When they believed that the resurrection took place in the lives of believers is not indicated, perhaps at baptism. They prob. based their teaching on a misinterpretation of Romans 6:1-11 and Colossians 3:1. It was motivated by incipient Gnosticism, which held that matter was evil and that consequently salvation consisted in liberation from the body. The teaching of a future bodily resurrection was deemed illogical and inconceivable (cf. 1 Cor 15:12). That Hymenaeus taught that the resurrection takes place in one's children is unlikely (cf. *Acts of Paul and Thecla* 2:14; Ecclus 30:4)."[11]

2. Philetus

The apostle speaks of Hymenaeus and Philetus as instances of men who were doing most serious injury to the church by their teaching, and by what that teaching resulted in, both in faith and morals. The specific error of these men was that they denied that there would be any bodily resurrection. They treated all Scriptural references to such a state as figurative or metaphorical. They spiritualized it absolutely, and held that the resurrection was a thing of the past. No resurrection was possible, so they taught, except from ignorance to

---

[11] 1. Hymenaeus - Encyclopedia of the bible - bible gateway, accessed February 19, 2024, https://www.biblegateway.com/resources/encyclopedia-of-the-bible/Hymenaeus.

knowledge, from sin to righteousness. There would be no day when the dead would hear the voice of Christ and come forth out of the grave. The Christian, knowing that Christ was raised from the dead, looked forward to the day when his body should be raised in the likeness of Christ's resurrection. But this faith was utterly denied by the teaching of Hymeneus and Philetus.

This teaching of theirs, Paul tells us, had overthrown the faith of some. It would also overthrow Christian faith altogether, for if the dead are not raised, neither is Christ risen from the dead, and "ye are yet in your sins"

The denial of the resurrection of the body, whether of mankind generally or of Christ, is the overthrow of the faith. It leaves nothing to cling to, no living Christ, who saves and leads and comforts His people. The apostle proceeds to say that teaching of this kind "eats as doth a gangrene," and that it increases unto more ungodliness. As a <u>canker</u> or <u>gangrene</u> eats away the flesh, so does such teaching eat away Christian faith. Paul is careful to say, more than once, that the teaching which denies that there will be a resurrection of the dead leads inevitably to "ungodliness" and to "iniquity."

Hymenaeus and Philetus may have believed in a nascent form of the Christian <u>heresy</u> of <u>Gnosticism</u>."[12]

---

[12] 1. "Philetus (Biblical Figure)," Wikipedia, September 19, 2021, https://en.wikipedia.org/wiki/Philetus_(biblical_figure).

Culture Section

Questioning the passage

1. Why does Paul refer to Timothy as his son? (v. 1)

    Elderly men and teachers in the near East use the term son as a term of endearment. It also is a sign that Timothy was a student of Paul.

2. What does verse twenty mean?

    Kings, princes, and rich man in Paul's day use vessels of pure gold and silver. The gold and silver vessels were used at banquets and state dinners, and only used by the owner. In this way, the owner could show his wealth to his guests. The ordinary pottery and wooden vessels were used for the servants and, if unimportant, guests were at the house for dinner. Regarding this verse, Paul encouraged Christians to purge themselves of any habits that were harmful. They were to become pure like gold vessels and ready to serve Yeshua.

Thoughts

Paul emphasizes in this chapter that it is his form of Christianity that must be followed. He lets Timothy know that there will be others that will try to change him. Today we can see that when a Catholic priest tells his congregation that if they take communion outside of the Catholic Church that they're destined to hell. They are not the only denomination who does that. Each denomination feels that it has the exclusive answer to what Yeshua taught us in the Gospels. It is said that in the 1880s the world church organization commissioned a group of theologians to determine what communion meant. They were hopeful that one answer would come out. To their dismay the theologians came out with several possible answers to what the meaning of communion is. Perhaps it comes down to the fact that one must believe what one feels is right.

1. What does it mean to hold onto godliness by denying its power? (v. 5)

2. Jannes and Jambres

3. Compare Paul's way to not Paul's way

4. What happened at Anitioch, Iconium, and Lystra

5. Why did those who followers Christ Jesus been persecuted? (v. 12)

6. Who are the imposters/evil men? (v. 13)

7. What was the Scripture Paul refers to in verse sixteen?

8. Did the Gentiles know about the Hebrew Scripture/prophets?

Chapter Three

Language

Peshitta	New American Standard 1995
2Timothy 3:1 But this know thou, that in the latter days hard times will come: **2** and men will be lovers of themselves, and lovers of money, boasters, proud, censorious, unyielding towards their own people, denyers of grace, wicked, **3** calumniators, addicted to concupiscence, ferocious, haters of the good, **4** treacherous, rash, inflated, attached to pleasure more than to the love of God, **5** having a form of respect for God, but wide from the power of God. Them who are such, repel from thee. **6** For of them are they who creep into this and that house, and captivate the women who are plunged in sins and led away by divers lusts, **7** who are always learning, and can never come to the knowledge of the truth. **8** Now as Jannes and Jambres withstood Moses, so also do these withstand the truth: men whose mind is corrupted, and [they] reprobates from the faith. **9** But they will not make progress, for their infatuation will be understood by every one, as theirs also was understood. **10** But thou hast followed after my doctrine, and my manner of life, and my aims, and my faith, and my long suffering, and my love, and my patience, **11** and my persecution, and my sufferings. And thou knowest what I endured at Antioch, and at Iconium, and at Lystra; what persecution I endured: and from all these my Lord delivered me. **12** And likewise all, who	**2Timothy 3:1** But realize this, that [a]in the last days difficult times will come. **2** For men will be [a]lovers of self, [b]lovers of money, [c]boastful, [c]arrogant, [d]revilers, [e]disobedient to parents, [e]ungrateful, [f]unholy, **3** [a]unloving, irreconcilable, [b]malicious gossips, without self-control, brutal, [1a]haters of good, **4** [a]treacherous, [b]reckless, [c]conceited, [d]lovers of pleasure rather than lovers of God, **5** holding to a form of [1a]godliness, although they have [b]denied its power; [c]Avoid such men as these. **6** For among them are those who [1a]enter into households and captivate [2b]weak women weighed down with sins, led on by [c]various impulses, **7** always learning and never able to [a]come to the [1]knowledge of the truth. **8** Just as [a]Jannes and Jambres [b]opposed Moses, so these *men* also oppose the truth, [c]men of depraved mind, rejected in regard to the faith. **9** But they will not make further progress; for their [a]folly will be obvious to all, just [b]as [1]Jannes's and Jambres's folly was also. **2Timothy 3:10** Now you [a]followed my teaching, conduct, purpose, faith, patience, [b]love, [1]perseverance, **11** [a]persecutions, *and* [b]sufferings, such as happened to me at [c]Antioch, at [d]Iconium *and* at [e]Lystra; what [f]persecutions I endured, and out of them all [g]the Lord rescued me! **12** Indeed, all who desire to live godly in Christ Jesus [a]will be

choose to live in the fear of God, in Jesus the Messiah, will be persecuted. **13** But evil and seducing men will add to their wickedness, while they deceive and are deceived. **14** But continue thou in the things thou hast learned and been assured of; for thou knowest from whom thou learnedst; **15** because from thy childhood, thou wast taught the holy books, which can make thee wise unto life, by faith in Jesus the Messiah. **16** All scripture that was written by the Spirit, is profitable for instruction, and for confutation, and for correction, and for erudition in righteousness; **17** that the man of God may become perfect, and complete for every good work.

persecuted. **13** But evil men and impostors *[a]*will proceed *from bad* to worse, *[b]*deceiving and being deceived. **14** You, however, *[a]*continue in the things you have learned and become convinced of, knowing from whom you have learned *them,* **15** and that *[a]*from childhood you have known *[b]*the sacred writings which are able to *[c]*give you the wisdom that leads to *[d]*salvation through faith which is in *[e]*Christ Jesus. **16** *[a]*All Scripture is *[1]*inspired by God and profitable for teaching, for reproof, for correction, for *[2]*training in righteousness; **17** so that *[a]*the man of God may be adequate, *[b]*equipped for every good work.

2Timothy 3:1
[a]1 Tim 4:1

2Timothy 3:2
[a]Phil 2:21
[b]Luke 16:14; 1 Tim 3:3; 6:10
[c]Rom 1:30
[d]2 Pet 2:10-12
[e]Luke 6:35
[f]1 Tim 1:9

2Timothy 3:3
[1]Lit *not loving good*
[a]Rom 1:31
[b]1 Tim 3:11
[c]Titus 1:8

2Timothy 3:4
[a]Acts 7:52
[b]Acts 19:36
[c]1 Tim 3:6
[d]Phil 3:19

2Timothy 3:5
[1]Or *religion*
[a]1 Tim 4:7
[b]1 Tim 5:8
[c]Matt 7:15; 2 Thess 3:6

2Timothy 3:6
[1]Or *creep into*
[2]Or *idle*
[a]Jude 4
[b]1 Tim 5:6; Titus 3:3
[c]Titus 3:3

2Timothy 3:7

[1]Or *recognition*
[a]2 Tim 2:25

2Timothy 3:8
[a]Ex 7:11
[b]Acts 13:8
[c]1 Tim 6:5

2Timothy 3:9
[1]Lit *that of those*
[a]Luke 6:11
[b]Ex 7:11, 12; 8:18; 9:11

2Timothy 3:10
[1]Or *steadfastness*
[a]Phil 2:20, 22; 1 Tim 4:6
[b]1 Tim 6:11

2Timothy 3:11
[a]2 Cor 12:10
[b]2 Cor 1:5, 7
[c]Acts 13:14, 45, 50
[d]Acts 14:1-7, 19
[e]Acts 14:8-20
[f]2 Cor 11:23-27
[g]Rom 15:31

2Timothy 3:12
[a]John 15:20; Acts 14:22; 2 Cor 4:9f

2Timothy 3:13
[a]2 Tim 2:16
[b]Titus 3:3

2Timothy 3:14
[a]2 Tim 1:13; Titus 1:9

2Timothy 3:15
[a]2 Tim 1:5
[b]John 5:47; Rom 2:27
[c]Ps 119:98f

[d]1 Cor 1:21
[e]2 Tim 1:1

2 Timothy 3:16

[1]Lit *God-breathed*
[2]Lit *training which is in*
[a]Rom 4:23f; 15:4; 2 Pet 1:20f

2 Timothy 3:17

[a]1 Tim 6:11
[b]2 Tim 2:21; Heb 13:21

2Timothy 3:1 Τοῦτο δὲ γίνωσκε, ὅτι ἐν ἐσχάταις ἡμέραις ἐνστήσονται καιροὶ χαλεποί. **2** Ἔσονται γὰρ οἱ ἄνθρωποι φίλαυτοι, φιλάργυροι, ἀλαζόνες, ὑπερήφανοι, βλάσφημοι, γονεῦσιν ἀπειθεῖς, ἀχάριστοι, ἀνόσιοι, **3** ἄστοργοι, ἄσπονδοι, διάβολοι, ἀκρατεῖς, ἀνήμεροι, ἀφιλάγαθοι, **4** προδόται, προπετεῖς, τετυφωμένοι, φιλήδονοι μᾶλλον ἢ φιλόθεοι, **5** ἔχοντες μόρφωσιν εὐσεβείας, τὴν δὲ δύναμιν αὐτῆς ἠρνημένοι· καὶ τούτους ἀποτρέπου. **6** Ἐκ τούτων γάρ εἰσιν οἱ ἐνδύνοντες εἰς τὰς οἰκίας, καὶ αἰχμαλωτεύοντες γυναικάρια σεσωρευμένα ἁμαρτίαις, ἀγόμενα ἐπιθυμίαις ποικίλαις, **7** πάντοτε μανθάνοντα, καὶ μηδέποτε εἰς ἐπίγνωσιν ἀληθείας ἐλθεῖν δυνάμενα. **8** Ὃν τρόπον δὲ Ἰαννῆς καὶ Ἰαμβρῆς ἀντέστησαν Μωϋσῇ, οὕτως καὶ οὗτοι ἀνθίστανται τῇ ἀληθείᾳ, ἄνθρωποι κατεφθαρμένοι τὸν νοῦν, ἀδόκιμοι περὶ τὴν πίστιν. **9** Ἀλλ' οὐ προκόψουσιν ἐπὶ πλεῖον· ἡ γὰρ ἄνοια αὐτῶν ἔκδηλος ἔσται πᾶσιν, ὡς καὶ ἡ ἐκείνων ἐγένετο. **10** Σὺ δὲ παρηκολούθηκάς μου τῇ διδασκαλίᾳ, τῇ ἀγωγῇ, τῇ προθέσει, τῇ πίστει, τῇ μακροθυμίᾳ, τῇ ἀγάπῃ, τῇ ὑπομονῇ, **11** τοῖς διωγμοῖς, τοῖς παθήμασιν, οἷά μοι ἐγένετο ἐν Ἀντιοχείᾳ, ἐν Ἰκονίῳ, ἐν Λύστροις, οἵους διωγμοὺς ὑπήνεγκα· καὶ ἐκ πάντων με ἐρρύσατο ὁ κύριος. **12** Καὶ πάντες δὲ οἱ θέλοντες εὐσεβῶς ζῆν ἐν χριστῷ Ἰησοῦ διωχθήσονται. **13** Πονηροὶ δὲ ἄνθρωποι καὶ γόητες προκόψουσιν ἐπὶ τὸ χεῖρον, πλανῶντες καὶ πλανώμενοι. **14** Σὺ δὲ μένε ἐν οἷς ἔμαθες καὶ ἐπιστώθης, εἰδὼς παρὰ τίνος ἔμαθες, **15** καὶ ὅτι ἀπὸ βρέφους τὰ ἱερὰ γράμματα οἶδας, τὰ δυνάμενά σε σοφίσαι εἰς σωτηρίαν διὰ πίστεως τῆς ἐν χριστῷ Ἰησοῦ. **16** Πᾶσα γραφὴ θεόπνευστος καὶ ὠφέλιμος πρὸς διδασκαλίαν, πρὸς ἔλεγχον, πρὸς ἐπανόρθωσιν, πρὸς παιδείαν τὴν ἐν δικαιοσύνῃ· **17** ἵνα ἄρτιος ᾖ ὁ τοῦ θεοῦ ἄνθρωπος, πρὸς πᾶν ἔργον ἀγαθὸν ἐξηρτισμένος.

Language

Process of Discovery

Linguistics Section

Linguistic Structure

Discussion

Questioning the Passage

1. What does it mean to hold on to godliness by denying its power? (v. 5)

    To deny the power of godliness while holding on to it means to outwardly appear religious or pious, following certain rituals or practices associated with faith, but not truly experiencing or demonstrating the transformative power of a genuine relationship with God. It suggests that such individuals may go through the motions of religion but lack genuine faith or spiritual vitality. They may adhere to religious traditions or cultural norms without experiencing the life-changing impact of God's presence in their lives.

    This verse warns against hypocrisy and superficiality in religious practice. It encourages believers to seek not just the outward appearance of godliness but also the inward transformation that comes from a sincere faith in God and reliance on His power to change lives.

2. What is the difference between Paul's way and the other ways?

    Paul determined what he fell Christianity was going to be. He determined what Yeshua's mission in life was. Since there were no gospel stories written Paul developed his own gospel. The major adversary to Paul's way with the Gnostics from Northern Egypt. The Gnostics believed the Messiah brought the secret knowledge from God back to earth. That secret knowledge was given to Moses on Mount Sinai. Over the centuries, the secret knowledge has been lost. The actual secret knowledge is to love God and to love neighbor. For the Gnostics, Yeshua gave up his life because he was a man of peace and evil world. He is the Messiah because he gave us the secret knowledge that was lost.

Paul converted Mithras House churches into Yeshua house churches. He collected the Mithras cult beliefs about the Messiah and applied them to Yeshua. In the Mithras cult, it was believed that Mithras died for the forgiveness of the sin of his followers. This is just one of numerous beliefs that came from the Mithras cult and Paul incorporated them into his form of Christianity because it made it easier to convert the Mithras house churches into Yeshua house churches. 90% of Christian rituals were originally Mithras Cult rituals (refer to Mike's book titled "Christianity's Need for Mithras."

Paul constantly in his letters reminded his followers that they need to follow his former Christianity and no other.

3. What happened at Antioch, Iconium, and Lystra? (v. 11)
Antioch: This was a city near Pisidia. Paul and Barnabas visited Antioch during their first missionary journey (Acts 13:14-52). They preached the gospel in the synagogue but faced opposition from some Jews who stirred up persecution against them. Paul and Barnabas were eventually expelled from the city.

Iconium: After being expelled from Antioch, Paul and Barnabas traveled to Iconium (Acts 14:1-7). There, they continued to preach the gospel, and many

Jews and Gentiles believed. However, opposition arose again, and there was a plot to mistreat and stone them. Faced with this threat, Paul and Barnabas fled to Lystra and Derbe.

Lystra: Lystra was the next stop on Paul and Barnabas's journey (Acts 14:8-21). In Lystra, Paul performed a miraculous healing, which led the people to believe that he and Barnabas were gods in human form. However, when Paul preached the gospel, some Jews from Antioch and Iconium stirred up the crowd against him. Paul was stoned and left for dead outside the city. Despite this, he later recovered and continued his missionary work.

4. Why did those who followers Christ Jesus been persecuted? (v. 12)
Early Christians faced persecution for several reasons:

1. Religious intolerance: The Roman Empire was highly religiously diverse, but it was also deeply intolerant of religions that refused to assimilate into the imperial cult. Christians were perceived as a threat because they refused to worship the Roman gods or the emperor. This refusal was seen as unpatriotic and a potential source of divine anger, leading to various calamities.

2. Social and cultural tensions: Christianity challenged the social norms and cultural practices of the time. It advocated for values such as humility, love, and equality that were often at odds with the hierarchical and often brutal social structures of the Roman world. As a result, Christians were sometimes viewed as subversive or destabilizing elements in society.

3. Misunderstandings and rumors: Early Christians were often misunderstood and accused of engaging in immoral or subversive practices, such as cannibalism (due to the ritual of the Eucharist) or incest (because Christians referred to each other as "brothers" and "sisters"). These misunderstandings fueled suspicion and hostility toward the Christian community.

4. Scapegoating: During times of crisis or hardship, Christians were sometimes scapegoated for societal problems. For example, when natural disasters or political unrest occurred, Christians were sometimes blamed, as their refusal to participate in traditional religious rituals was seen as angering the gods and bringing divine punishment.

5. Political tensions: Christianity's refusal to worship the emperor as a god and its insistence on the kingship of Jesus Christ were seen as challenges to imperial authority. This led to conflicts with the state, particularly during periods of intense imperial persecution, such as under emperors like Nero and Diocletian.

Overall, early Christians faced persecution due to a combination of religious, social, cultural, and political factors, all of which contributed to their marginalization and often brutal treatment by the authorities and broader society.

5. Who are the imposters/evil men? (v. 13)
The imposters were people who had a different understanding of Christianity and wanted to convince the people in the churches of Asia Minor to follow their former Christianity and abandon Paul's.

6. What was the Scripture Paul refers to in verse sixteen?

Second Timothy 3:16 is a verse from the New Testament of the Bible, specifically from the Second Epistle of Paul to Timothy. It states:

"All Scripture is God-breathed and is useful for teaching, rebuking, correcting and training in righteousness," (2 Timothy 3:16, NIV).

This verse emphasizes the divine inspiration and authority of Scripture. Here's a breakdown of its meaning:

1. All Scripture is God-breathed: This phrase asserts that every part of the Bible, both Old Testament and New Testament, originates from God. It implies that the writings of the Bible are not merely the product of human authors, but they were inspired by God himself. The term "God-breathed" suggests that the Holy Spirit guided the writers of Scripture, influencing what they wrote to ensure its accuracy and truthfulness.

2. Useful for teaching, rebuking, correcting, and training in righteousness: This part of the verse explains the purpose or utility of Scripture. It highlights that the Bible is not just a historical document or a collection of religious texts, but it serves practical functions in the lives of believers. It is useful for teaching, providing guidance and instruction in matters of faith and conduct. It also serves to rebuke, indicating errors or sin in one's life. It corrects, offering guidance on how to live rightly before God. Finally, it trains in righteousness, helping believers grow in their understanding of God's will and leading them to live righteous lives according to his standards.

In summary, 2 Timothy 3:16 affirms the divine authority and usefulness of Scripture for guiding and shaping the lives of believers, providing them with instruction, correction, and training in righteousness.

7. Did the Gentiles know about the Hebrew Scripture/prophets?

In the book of Ezekiel, it describes the people that were present in the fall of Jerusalem. One person was the head of the Magi. That individual would have come from the area of the Persian Empire. It is known that several of the Isaiah scrolls were taken back to Persia. Since the Magi came to visit the infant Yeshua according to Matthew's Gospel this proves that they knew what the Hebrew Scripture prophets were discussing.

Biblical Personalities

1. JANNES AND JAMBRES jăn' ĭz, jăm' brĭz (Ἰαννῆς καὶ Ἰαμβρῆς, or Μαμβρῆς, cited by a few MSS; for יֹּוחָנִי וּמַמְרֵא; Aram. Targ. ינים וימברים, possible meaning: *he who seduces* and *he who makes rebellious*). Traditional names of Egyp. sorcerers who opposed Moses before Pharaoh (2 Tim 3:8); evidently a reference back to unnamed magicians in the OT (Exod 7:11, 12, 22).

In the Exodus narrative, Moses and Aaron delivered to Pharaoh the Lord's message that Israel be allowed to go into the wilderness to worship God, and the monarch refused (Exod 5:1-4). Then Moses performed authenticating miracles, such as making his rod a serpent, which the sorcerers with their magic also did (Exod 7:10-12, 20-22; 8:5-7, 17, 18). It is to this series of events that Paul is referring in 2 Timothy 3:8.

The orthography of the names, Jannes and Jambres, is rather confused. The spelling in the Gr. texts is generally Ἰαννῆς and Ἰαμβρῆς, G2612, (corresponding to the *Targum of Jonathan* on Exod 1:15; 7:11; Num 22:22, which has *Yanis* and *Yambris*). The Talmud, however, has *Yôhanî* and *Mamre'*, and the Lat. reading is *Jannes* (or *Jamnes*) and *Mambres*.

These two names are mentioned in Scripture only in 2 Timothy 3:8 and are evidently connected with Jewish tradition. The names are also mentioned in pagan and early Christian lit. These terms are either thought of as a part of Jewish oral tradition, or connected with a book that had the title *Jamnes et Mambres*, as mentioned by Origen (*Tract* 35 in *Matt.*) and in the *Decretum Gelasii* (Credner, p. 220). Schürer (HJP, sec. div., III, p. 149) refers to a Jewish apocryphal work bearing both of these names, but which had disappeared except for the title and which he thinks may have been composed in pre-Christian times because the name Jannes was known by Pliny in the 1st cent.

Besides being mentioned in the Jewish *Targum of Jonathan*, and the *Talmud*, pagan writers knew of these two names. Both Pliny the Elder (1st cent. A.D.) in his *Historia Natural* 30, 1, 11 and Apuleius (2nd cent. A.D.) in his *Apologia* (or *De Magia*) ch. 90, refer to Jannes, whereas the neo-Platonist Numenius of Apamea (2nd cent. A.D.) referred to in Eusebius, *Praeparatio Evangelica* 9, 8, 1, was acquainted with both Jannes and Jambres, calling them holy scribes and magicians of Egypt.

Among materials connected with the Church and written in the early Christian centuries where reference is made to the names, Jannes and Jambres, are mentioned in such Gr. works as *Evangelium Nicodemi* (*Acta Pilati*) ch. 5, and the *Apostolic Constitution* 8, 1, and Lat. works as *Evangelium Nicodemi* (*Gesta Pilati*), ch. 5 and Cyprian, *De unitate ecclesia*, ch. 16.

That Paul mentions these traditional names in 2 Timothy 3:8 evidences his acquaintance with this current Jewish tradition (he was a student of Gamaliel, Acts 22:3) and, by using these terms (which could have been accurately passed down from OT history), Paul seemingly demonstrates his desire to make vivid the personal and forceful opposition of the Egyp. magician class against Moses. The Jewish tradition about Jannes and Jambres is confused as shown by Eusebius' statement (*Praeparatio Evangelica* 9, 8) that these two men were sons of Baalim but yet teachers of Moses and then his opponents, who then died with the Egyp. army in the Red Sea."[13]

---

[13] 1. Jannes and jambres - encyclopedia of the bible - bible gateway, accessed February 28, 2024, https://www.biblegateway.com/resources/encyclopedia-of-the-bible/Jannes-Jambres.

Biblical Locations

1. Antioch

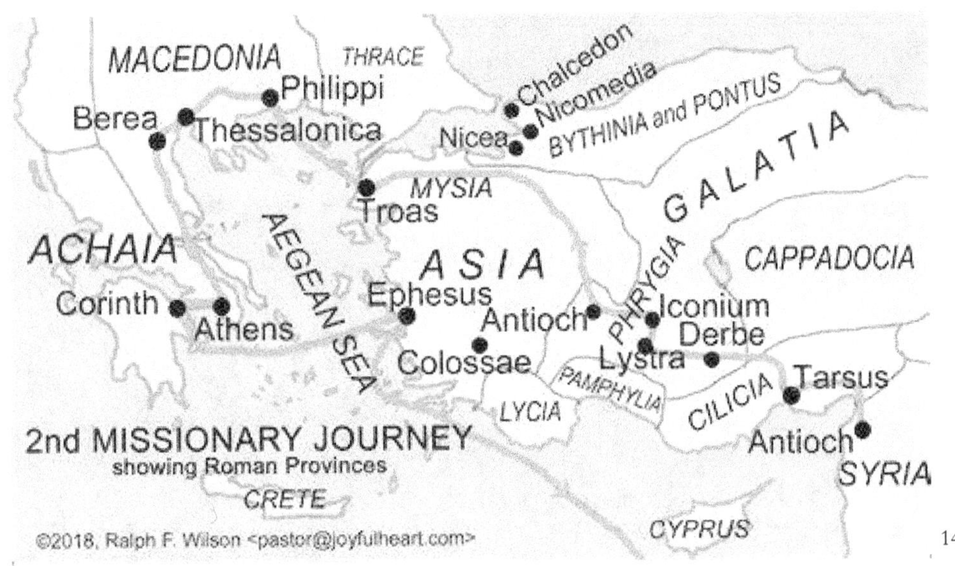

---

[14] 1. "5. Paul in Macedonia (Acts 15:36-18:22, 49-50 AD)," 5. Paul in Macedonia (Acts 15:36-18:22, 49-50 AD) -- Apostle Paul: Passsionate Discipleship, accessed February 28, 2024, https://www.jesuswalk.com/paul/05_macedonia.htm.

2. Iconium

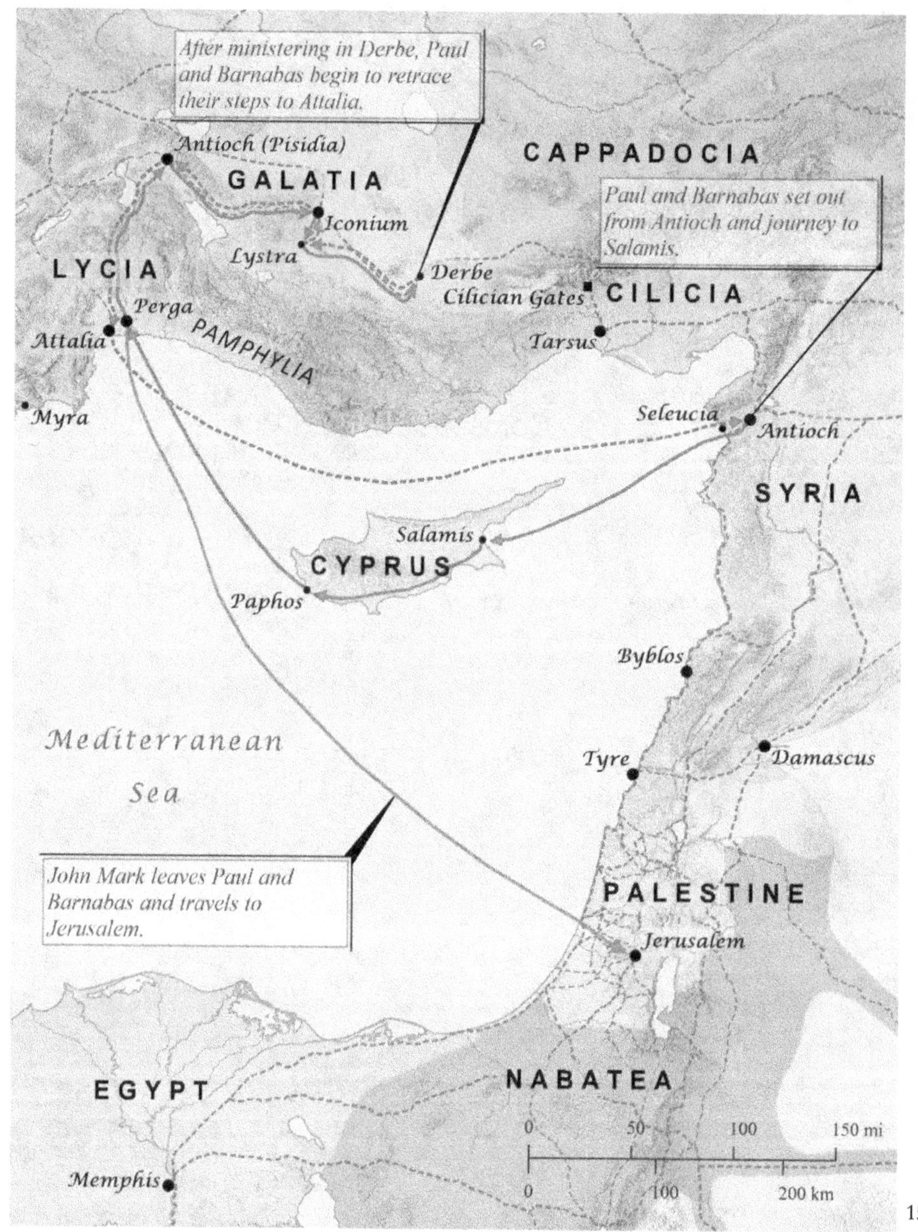

---

¹⁵ 1. Posted byAdministrator, "Paul's First Missionary Journey," Bible Mapper Atlas, January 15, 2024, https://biblemapper.com/blog/index.php/2020/02/13/southern-galatia/.

3. Lystra

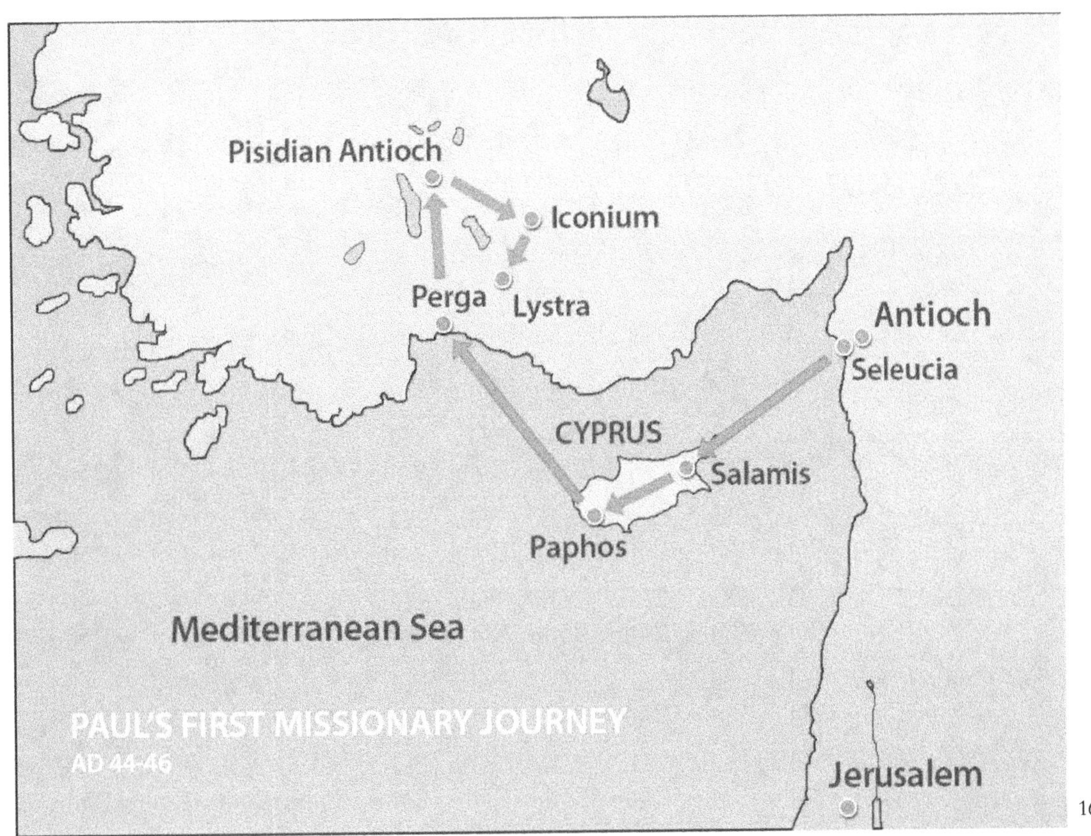

Thoughts

In this chapter, Paul continues to express his concerns that the Gnostics and other forms of Christianity might come into Asia minor to undermine his work.

---

[16] 1. "Paul and Barnabas in Lystra and Derbe :: Paul and Barnabas Visit Lystra and Derbe (Acts 14:8-28)," FreeBibleimages, accessed February 28, 2024, https://freebibleimages.org/illustrations/paul-lystra-derbe/.

Chapter Four

Language

Peshitta	New American Standard 1995
2Tim. 4:1 I charge thee, before God, and our Lord Jesus the Messiah, who is to judge the living and the dead, at the manifestation of his kingdom, **2** Proclaim the word; and persist [in it] with diligence, in time and out of time; admonish, and rebuke, with all patience and instructiveness. **3** For the time will come, when they will not give ear to sound teaching; but, according to their lusts, will multiply to themselves teachers, in the itching of their hearing; **4** and will turn away their ears from the truth, and incline after fables. **5** But be thou vigilant in all things; and endure evils, and do the work of an evangelist, and fulfill thy ministry. **6** But I am soon to be immolated; and the time of my dissolution hath come. **7** I have fought a good combat, I have completed my race, I have preserved my fidelity; **8** and henceforth there is preserved for me a crown of righteousness, with which my Lord, the righteous Judge, will recompense me in that day; and not me only, but them also who love his manifestation. **9** Exert thyself to come to me quickly. **10** For Demas hath left me; and hath loved this world and gone away to Thessalonica; Crispus to Galatia, Titus to Dalmatia. **11** Luke only is with me. Take Mark, and bring him with thee; for he is suitable for me, for ministration. **12** And Tychicus I have sent to Ephesus. **13** And when thou comest, bring the bookcase,	**2Tim. 4:1** *a*I solemnly charge *you* in the presence of God and of Christ Jesus, who is to *b*judge the living and the dead, and by His *c*appearing and His kingdom: **2** preach *a*the word; be ready in season *and* out of season; *b*reprove, rebuke, exhort, with *1*great *c*patience and instruction. **3** For *a*the time will come when they will not endure *b*sound doctrine; but *wanting* to have their ears tickled, they will accumulate for themselves teachers in accordance to their own desires, **4** and *a*will turn away their ears from the truth and *b*will turn aside to myths. **5** But you, *a*be sober in all things, *b*endure hardship, do the work of an *c*evangelist, fulfill your *d*ministry. **2Tim. 4:6** For I am already being *a*poured out as a drink offering, and the time of *b*my departure has come. **7** *a*I have fought the good fight, I have finished *b*the course, I have kept *c*the faith; **8** in the future there *a*is laid up for me *b*the crown of righteousness, which the Lord, the righteous Judge, will award to me on *c*that day; and not only to me, but also to *d*all who have loved His *e*appearing. **2Tim. 4:9** *a*Make every effort to come to me soon; **10** for *a*Demas, having loved *b*this present *1*world, has deserted me and gone to *c*Thessalonica; Crescens *has gone* to *2d*Galatia, *e*Titus to Dalmatia. **11** *a*Only *b*Luke is with me. Pick up *c*Mark and bring him

which I left at Troas with Carpus, and the books, but especially the roll of parchments. **14** Alexander the coppersmith showed me many ills: our Lord will reward him according to his doings. **15** And do thou also beware of him; for he is very insolent against our words. **16** At my first defence, no one was with me, but they all forsook me. Let not this be reckoned to them. **17** But my Lord stood by me, and strengthened me; that by me the preaching might be fulfilled; and [that] all the Gentiles might hear: and I was rescued from the mouth of the lion. **18** And my Lord will rescue me from every evil work; and will give me life in his heavenly kingdom. To him be glory, for ever and ever. Amen. **19** Present a salutation to Priscilla and Aquila, and to the household of Onesiphorus. **20** Erastus hath stopped at Corinth; and Trophimus I left sick at the city of Miletus. **21** Exert thyself to come before winter. Eubulus saluteth thee, and Pudens, and Linus, and Claudia, and all the brethren. **22** Our Lord Jesus the Messiah be with thy spirit. Grace be with thee. Amen.

with you, *d*for he is useful to me for service. **12** But *a*Tychicus I have sent to *b*Ephesus. **13** When you come bring the cloak which I left at *a*Troas with Carpus, and the books, especially the parchments. **14** *a*Alexander the coppersmith did me much harm; *b*the Lord will repay him according to his deeds. **15** Be on guard against him yourself, for he vigorously opposed our *1*teaching.

2Tim. 4:16 At my first defense no one supported me, but all deserted me; *a*may it not be counted against them. **17** But the Lord stood with me and *a*strengthened me, so that through me *b*the proclamation might *1*be *c*fully accomplished, and that all *d*the Gentiles might hear; and I was *e*rescued out of *f*the lion's mouth. **18** The Lord will rescue me from every evil deed, and will *1a*bring me safely to His *b*heavenly kingdom; *c*to *2*Him *be* the glory forever and ever. Amen.

2Tim. 4:19 Greet Prisca and *a*Aquila, and *b*the household of Onesiphorus. **20** *a*Erastus remained at *b*Corinth, but *c*Trophimus I left sick at *d*Miletus. **21** *a*Make every effort to come before *b*winter. Eubulus greets you, also Pudens and Linus and Claudia and all the brethren.

2Tim. 4:22 *a*The Lord be with your spirit. *b*Grace be with you.

2Timothy 4:1
[a]1 Tim 5:21; 2 Tim 2:14
[b]Acts 10:42
[c]2 Thess 2:8; 2 Tim 1:10; 4:8

2Timothy 4:2
[1]Lit *all*
[a]Gal 6:6; Col 4:3; 1 Thess 1:6
[b]1 Tim 5:20; Titus 1:13; 2:15
[c]2 Tim 3:10

2Timothy 4:3
[a]2 Tim 3:1
[b]1 Tim 1:10; 2 Tim 1:13

2Timothy 4:4
[a]2 Thess 2:11; Titus 1:14
[b]1 Tim 1:4

2Timothy 4:5
[a]1 Pet 1:13
[b]2 Tim 1:8
[c]Acts 21:8
[d]Eph 4:12; Col 4:17

2Timothy 4:6
[a]Phil 2:17
[b]Phil 1:23; 2 Pet 1:14

2Timothy 4:7
[a]1 Cor 9:25f; Phil 1:30; 1 Tim 1:18; 6:12
[b]Acts 20:24; 1 Cor 9:24
[c]2 Tim 3:10

2Timothy 4:8
[a]Col 1:5; 1 Pet 1:4
[b]1 Cor 9:25; 2 Tim 2:5; James 1:12

[c]2 Tim 1:12
[d]Phil 3:11
[e]2 Tim 4:1

2Timothy 4:9
[a]2 Tim 1:4; 4:21; Titus 3:12

2Timothy 4:10
[1]Or *age*
[2]One early ms reads *Gaul*
[a]Col 4:14
[b]1 Tim 6:17
[c]Acts 17:1
[d]Acts 16:6
[e]2 Cor 2:13; 8:23; Gal 2:3; Titus 1:4

2Timothy 4:11
[a]2 Tim 1:15
[b]Col 4:14; Philem 24
[c]Acts 12:12, 25; 15:37-39; Col 4:10
[d]2 Tim 2:21

2Timothy 4:12
[a]Acts 20:4; Eph 6:21, 22; Col 4:7f
[b]Acts 18:19

2Timothy 4:13
[a]Acts 16:8

2Timothy 4:14
[a]Acts 19:33; 1 Tim 1:20
[b]Ps 62:12; Rom 2:6; 12:19

2Timothy 4:15
[1]Lit *words*

2Timothy 4:16
[a]Acts 7:60; 1 Cor 13:5

2Timothy 4:17
[1]Or *be fulfilled*

[a]1 Tim 1:12; 2 Tim 2:1
[b]Titus 1:3
[c]2 Tim 4:5
[d]Acts 9:15; Phil 1:12ff
[e]Rom 15:31; 2 Tim 3:11
[f]1 Sam 17:37; Ps 22:21

2 Timothy 4:18
[1]Or *save me for*
[2]Lit *Whom*
[a]1 Cor 1:21
[b]1 Cor 15:50; 2 Tim 4:1; Heb 11:16; 12:22
[c]Rom 11:36; 2 Pet 3:18

2 Timothy 4:19
[a]Acts 18:2
[b]2 Tim 1:16

2 Timothy 4:20
[a]Acts 19:22; Rom 16:23
[b]Acts 18:1
[c]Acts 20:4; 21:29
[d]Acts 20:15

2 Timothy 4:21
[a]2 Tim 4:9
[b]Titus 3:12

2 Timothy 4:22
[a]Gal 6:18; Phil 4:23; Philem 25
[b]Col 4:18

2Tim. 4:1   Διαμαρτυρομαι ενωπιον του θεου και Χριστου Ιησου του μελλοντος κρινειν ζωντας και νεκρους, και την επιφανειαν αυτου και την βασιλειαν αυτου· [2] κηρυξον τον λογον, επιστηθι ευκαιρως ακαιρως, ελεγξον, επιτιμησον, παρακαλεσον, εν παση μακροθυμια και διδαχη. [3] Εσται γαρ καιρος οτε της υγιαινουσης διδασκαλιας ουκ ανεξονται αλλα κατα τας ιδιας επιθυμιας εαυτοις επισωρευσουσιν διδασκαλους κνηθομενοι την ακοην [4] και απο μεν της αληθειας την ακοην αποστρεφουσιν, επι δε τους μυθους εκτραπησονται. [5] Συ δε νηφε εν πασιν, κακοπαθησον, εργον ποιησον ευαγγελιστου, την διακονιαν σου πληροφορησον.

2Tim. 4:6   Εγω γαρ ηδη σπενδομαι, και ο καιρος της αναλυσεως μου εφεστηκεν. [7] τον καλον αγωνα ηγωνισμαι, τον δρομον τετελεκα, την πιστιν τετηρηκα· [8] λοιπον αποκειται μοι ο της δικαιοσυνης στεφανος, ον αποδωσει μοι ο κυριος εν εκεινη τη ημερα, ο δικαιος κριτης, ου μονον δε εμοι αλλα και πασιν τοις ηγαπηκοσιν την επιφανειαν αυτου.

2Tim. 4:9   Σπουδασον ελθειν προς με ταχεως· [10] Δημας γαρ με εγκατελιπεν αγαπησας τον νυν αιωνα και επορευθη εις Θεσσαλονικην, Κρησκης εις Γαλατιαν, Τιτος εις Δαλματιαν· [11] Λουκας εστιν μονος μετ᾽ εμου. Μαρκον αναλαβων αγε μετα σεαυτου, εστιν γαρ μοι ευχρηστος εις διακονιαν. [12] Τυχικον δε απεστειλα εις Εφεσον. [13] τον φαιλονην ον απελιπον εν Τρωαδι παρα Καρπω ερχομενος φερε, και τα βιβλια μαλιστα τας μεμβρανας. [14] Αλεξανδρος ο χαλκευς πολλα μοι κακα ενεδειξατο· αποδωσει αυτω ο κυριος κατα τα εργα αυτου· [15] ον και συ φυλασσου, λιαν γαρ αντεστη τοις ημετεροις λογοις. [16] Εν τη πρωτη μου απολογια ουδεις μοι παρεγενετο, αλλα παντες με εγκατελιπον· μη αυτοις λογισθειη· [17] ο δε κυριος μοι παρεστη και ενεδυναμωσεν με, ινα δι᾽ εμου το κηρυγμα πληροφορηθη και ακουσωσιν παντα τα εθνη, και ερρυσθην εκ στοματος λεοντος. [18] ρυσεται με ο κυριος απο παντος εργου πονηρου και σωσει εις την βασιλειαν αυτου την επουρανιον· ω η δοξα εις τους αιωνας των αιωνων, αμην.

2Tim. 4:19   Ασπασαι Πρισκαν και Ακυλαν και τον Ονησιφορου οικον. [20] Εραστος εμεινεν εν Κορινθω, Τροφιμον δε απελιπον εν Μιλητω ασθενουντα. [21] Σπουδασον προ χειμωνος ελθειν. Ασπαζεται σε Ευβουλος και Πουδης και Λινος και Κλαυδια και οι αδελφοι παντες.

2Tim. 4:22   Ο κυριος μετα του πνευματος σου. η χαρις μεθ᾽ υμων.

Language

  Process of Discovery

    Linguistics Section

      Linguistic Structure

[Paul's Charge] 1 *I solemnly charge *you* in the presence of God and of Christ Jesus, who is to *judge the living and the dead, and by His *appearing and His kingdom: **2** preach *the word; be ready in season *and* out of season; *reprove, rebuke, exhort, with great *patience and instruction. **3** For *the time will come when they will not endure *sound doctrine; but *wanting* to have their ears tickled, they will accumulate for themselves teachers in accordance to their own desires, **4** and *will turn away their ears from the truth and *will turn aside to myths. **5** But you, *be sober in all things, *endure hardship, do the work of an *evangelist, fulfill your *ministry.

[Paul believed his death was near] 6 For I am already being *poured out as a drink offering, and the time of *my departure has come. **7** *I have fought the good fight, I have finished *the course, I have kept *the faith; **8** in the future there *is laid up for me *the crown of righteousness, which the Lord, the righteous Judge, will award to me on *that day; and not only to me, but also to *all who have loved His *appearing.

[Paul's plea for a visit] 9 *Make every effort to come to me soon; **10** for *Demas, having loved *this present world, has deserted me and gone to *Thessalonica; Crescens *has gone* to *Galatia, *Titus to Dalmatia. **11** *Only *Luke is with me. Pick up *Mark and bring him with you, *for he is useful to me for service. **12** But *Tychicus I have sent to *Ephesus. **13** When you come bring the cloak which I left at *Troas with Carpus, and the books, especially the parchments. **14** *Alexander the coppersmith did me much harm; *the Lord will repay him according to his deeds. **15** Be on guard against him yourself, for he vigorously opposed our teaching.

[Supporters deserted him] 16 At my first defense no one supported me, but all deserted me; *may it not be counted against them. **17** But the Lord stood with me and *strengthened me, so that through me *the proclamation might be *fully accomplished, and that all *the Gentiles might hear; and I was *rescued out of *the lion's mouth. **18** The

Lord will rescue me from every evil deed, and will ¹ᵃbring me safely to His ᵇheavenly kingdom; ᶜto ²Him *be* the glory forever and ever. Amen.

[**Closing**] **19** Greet Prisca and ᵃAquila, and ᵇthe household of Onesiphorus. **20** ᵃErastus remained at ᵇCorinth, but ᶜTrophimus I left sick at ᵈMiletus. **21** ᵃMake every effort to come before ᵇwinter. Eubulus greets you, also Pudens and Linus and Claudia and all the brethren. **22** ᵃThe Lord be with your spirit. ᵇGrace be with you.

Discussion

This chapter is another expression of Paul's belief that he had the exclusive definition of Christianity.

Questioning the Passage

1. What does immolated mean? (v. 6)

   The term "immolated" refers to the act of sacrificing or killing someone, often as a religious ritual, by burning them alive or killing them in a sacrificial manner, typically as an offering to a deity or as a form of punishment. In a broader sense, it can also refer to sacrificing or destroying something valuable or cherished for a particular purpose or cause.

2. What is a drink offering? (v. 6)

   A drink offering, also known as a libation, is a ritual act of pouring out a liquid, such as wine, water, oil, or even blood, as an offering to a deity or spirit. This practice has been a part of various religious and cultural traditions throughout history.

In the context of ancient Israelite religion, drink offerings were often accompanied by other offerings, such as animal sacrifices, and were typically poured out at an altar as part of worship rituals. The liquid poured out was seen as symbolically representing the life force or essence of the offering, and it was believed to be a way of honoring the divine and seeking favor or blessings.

In the New Testament of the Christian Bible, references to drink offerings can be found, such as in Philippians 2:17 and 2 Timothy 4:6, where the Apostle Paul uses the imagery of his life being poured out like a drink offering in service to God. This reflects the concept of self-sacrifice and devotion to God's will.

3. What is a crown of righteousness? (v. 8)

In the context of Christian theology, a "crown of righteousness" is a metaphorical term used to describe a reward or honor that awaits faithful believers in heaven. It is often associated with the idea of receiving recognition or a special commendation from God for a life lived in accordance with His will and teachings.

The phrase "crown of righteousness" is derived from the New Testament, specifically from 2 Timothy 4:8, where the Apostle Paul writes:

"Henceforth there is laid up for me the crown of righteousness, which the Lord, the righteous judge, will award to me on that day, and not only to me but also to all who have loved his appearing." (ESV)

Here, Paul is expressing his confidence that, despite the challenges and trials he has faced in his ministry, he will be rewarded with a crown of righteousness from the Lord. This crown symbolizes the ultimate vindication and approval of his faithfulness and dedication to serving God.

In Christian theology, the concept of receiving a crown of righteousness is often linked to the broader idea of believers receiving rewards or crowns in heaven for their faithful service and devotion to God. It serves as an encouragement for Christians to persevere in their faith and to live righteous lives in anticipation of the eternal blessings promised by God.

4. What does it mean that Demas is in love with the present world? (v. 10)

Demas had previously been involved in Paul's ministry, had abandoned his service to Paul and the Gospel because he was more drawn to the attractions and pursuits of the world. The phrase "in love with this present world" indicates that Demas had become enamored or captivated by the worldly desires, pleasures, and distractions of the secular life.

Paul's mention of Demas serves as a warning about the dangers of becoming too attached to worldly pursuits and priorities at the expense of one's commitment to God and His kingdom. It highlights the importance of maintaining a steadfast devotion to Christ and His teachings, even when faced with the temptations and allurements of the world.

5. What are the books and parchments in verse thirteen?

Paul is asking Timothy to bring several items to him:

1. Cloak: This refers to a garment that Paul had left behind in Troas, which he likely needed for warmth or comfort, especially considering he was in prison and may have been experiencing hardship.

2. Books: The specific books Paul refers to are not mentioned, leaving the content open to interpretation. However, it's reasonable to assume that these were written materials, likely containing Scripture or other writings relevant to Paul's ministry or personal study.

3. Parchments: Parchments were writing materials made from animal skin, typically used for more important or permanent documents. In this context, the "parchments" likely refer to documents or writings of particular significance to Paul, perhaps including his own letters or copies of Scripture.

Paul's request for these items indicates his continued dedication to studying and teaching, even while imprisoned. It also provides insight into the practical aspects of his life and ministry, demonstrating his reliance on others, such as Timothy, for assistance and support.

6. Where is forgiveness in verse fourteen?

This verse is about Paul mentioning Alexander, who apparently caused him harm. Paul expresses confidence that God will deal with Alexander according to his actions. However, forgiveness as a concept is not specifically addressed in this verse. It primarily focuses on Paul's acknowledgment of the harm done to him and his trust in God's justice.

7. Does verse sixteen include Timothy?

This verse reflects Paul's experience during his trial or legal defense, where he felt abandoned by those who could have supported him. Despite feeling deserted, Paul expresses a forgiving attitude, asking that their abandonment not be held against them. It shows Paul's grace and willingness to forgive those who failed to support him in his time of need.

8. What does it mean to be rescued from the lion's mouth? (v. 17)

In this verse, Paul is expressing his gratitude and confidence in the Lord's faithfulness. Despite feeling abandoned by people during his trial or defense, Paul asserts that the Lord stood by him and provided him with strength. This divine support enabled Paul to continue proclaiming the message of the Gospel, particularly to the Gentiles, without hindrance.

The phrase "rescued from the lion's mouth" is likely a metaphorical expression, suggesting that Paul was delivered from a situation of extreme danger or threat. It could refer to his deliverance from persecution, imprisonment, or other perilous circumstances.

Overall, 2 Timothy 4:17 emphasizes Paul's reliance on God's presence and empowerment in the midst of adversity, highlighting the theme of divine assistance and provision throughout his ministry.

9. Why was it important to get to Paul before winter? (v. 21)

In 2 Timothy 4:21, Paul writes, "Do your best to come before winter. Eubulus sends greetings to you, as do Pudens and Linus and Claudia and all the brothers."

The importance of traveling before winter in this context likely reflects practical considerations related to the challenges and dangers of winter travel in the ancient world. Winter could bring harsh weather conditions, such as snowstorms, freezing temperatures, and icy roads, making travel difficult, slow, and potentially hazardous.

For Timothy, the recipient of Paul's letter, and for others who might be traveling to visit Paul or engage in ministry, it would have been important to plan their journey in such a way as to avoid the perils and delays associated with winter travel. Traveling before winter would have ensured a safer and more efficient journey, allowing them to reach their destination in a timely manner.

Additionally, visiting Paul before winter may have been particularly important due to his circumstances. As a prisoner, Paul's access to visitors and support may have been more restricted during the winter months, making it imperative for his companions to come to him before the onset of winter to provide assistance, encouragement, and fellowship.

Overall, the urgency of traveling before winter in 2 Timothy 4:21 underscores the practical considerations and logistical challenges faced by early Christians in their efforts to support one another and continue their ministry endeavors, even in the face of external obstacles such as seasonal weather conditions.

Biblical Personalities

1. Demas – Demas was a figure mentioned in the New Testament of the Bible. He is referred to in three of the Pauline epistles: Colossians, Philemon, and 2 Timothy. In Colossians 4:14, he is mentioned alongside Luke as one of Paul's fellow workers. However, in 2 Timothy 4:10, Paul writes that Demas has forsaken him, having loved the present world, and has departed for Thessalonica. This suggests a falling away from the Christian faith or from Paul's company due to worldly desires. The exact identity and further details about Demas are not provided in the biblical text, leaving much room for speculation and interpretation.

2. Crescens - Crescens is another figure mentioned in the New Testament of the Bible. He is referenced in 2 Timothy 4:10, where Paul writes, "for Demas, in love with this present world, has deserted me and gone to Thessalonica; Crescens has gone to Galatia, Titus to Dalmatia."

Like Demas, Crescens was one of Paul's associates or fellow workers in his missionary endeavors. The biblical text doesn't provide much detail about Crescens beyond this mention, so his exact role and identity are not well understood. Some traditions and interpretations suggest he might have been one of the early Christian missionaries who accompanied Paul in his travels.

However, beyond this brief reference, there isn't much historical information available about Crescens.

3. Titus - Titus was a prominent figure in the New Testament of the Bible, particularly in the writings of the apostle Paul. He is mentioned several times in the Pauline epistles.

Titus is believed to have been a Gentile Christian who became a close companion and collaborator of Paul. He is mentioned in Galatians, 2 Corinthians, and the pastoral epistles (1 Timothy and Titus). In these letters, Paul often refers to Titus as his "partner" or "fellow worker."

Titus played a significant role in Paul's missionary activities. He was entrusted with important tasks such as overseeing the collection for the poor Christians in Jerusalem (2 Corinthians 8:6) and handling various matters in the church in Corinth (2 Corinthians 7:6-7, 13-15).

Additionally, the Epistle to Titus is addressed to him, offering guidance on pastoral leadership and church administration. This indicates that Titus held a position of leadership and responsibility within the early Christian community.

Titus is depicted as a faithful and reliable companion of Paul, entrusted with important responsibilities in spreading the Christian message and nurturing the early church.

4. Luke - Luke, also known as Luke the Evangelist or Saint Luke, was a significant figure in early Christianity and the author of the Gospel of Luke and the Acts of the Apostles in the New Testament of the Bible.

Traditionally, Luke is considered to have been a physician and a Gentile Christian. He is believed to have been a close companion of the apostle Paul and accompanied him on some of his missionary journeys. References in Paul's letters suggest that Luke was with Paul during his imprisonment (Colossians 4:14; Philemon 1:24; 2 Timothy 4:11).

Luke's Gospel is known for its detailed and orderly account of the life, ministry, death, and resurrection of Jesus Christ. It emphasizes Jesus' compassion for the marginalized and includes unique stories and parables not found in the other Gospels.

The Acts of the Apostles, also written by Luke, narrates the early spread of Christianity after Jesus' ascension, focusing particularly on the ministry of the apostles Peter and Paul. It provides valuable historical and theological insights into the growth of the early Christian church, including the Day of Pentecost, the conversion of Saul (who later became the apostle Paul), and the missionary journeys of Paul.

Luke's contributions to the New Testament have had a profound influence on Christian theology and spirituality, and he is venerated as a saint in various Christian denominations.

5. Mark - Luke, also known as Luke the Evangelist or Saint Luke, was a significant figure in early Christianity and the author of the Gospel of Luke and the Acts of the Apostles in the New Testament of the Bible.

Traditionally, Luke is considered to have been a physician and a Gentile Christian. He is believed to have been a close companion of the apostle Paul and accompanied him on some of his missionary journeys. References in Paul's letters suggest that Luke was with Paul during his imprisonment (Colossians 4:14; Philemon 1:24; 2 Timothy 4:11).

Luke's Gospel is known for its detailed and orderly account of the life, ministry, death, and resurrection of Jesus Christ. It emphasizes Jesus' compassion for the marginalized and includes unique stories and parables not found in the other Gospels.

The Acts of the Apostles, also written by Luke, narrates the early spread of Christianity after Jesus' ascension, focusing particularly on the ministry of the apostles Peter and Paul. It provides valuable historical and theological insights into the growth of the early Christian church, including the Day of Pentecost, the conversion of Saul (who later became the apostle Paul), and the missionary journeys of Paul.

Luke's contributions to the New Testament have had a profound influence on Christian theology and spirituality, and he is venerated as a saint in various Christian denominations.

6. Tychicus - Tychicus was a companion and fellow worker of the apostle Paul, mentioned several times in the New Testament. He played various supportive roles in Paul's ministry and the early Christian community.

In the New Testament, Tychicus is mentioned in the following passages:

1. Acts 20:4: Tychicus is listed as one of the companions of Paul during his travels.

2. Ephesians 6:21: In this passage, Tychicus is described as a beloved brother and faithful minister in the Lord. He is mentioned as the one whom Paul sent to the Ephesian church to provide information about Paul's circumstances and to encourage them.

3. Colossians 4:7: Tychicus is described similarly in this passage, as a beloved brother, faithful minister, and fellow servant in the Lord. He is mentioned as the one whom Paul sent to the church in Colossae to provide information about Paul's circumstances and to encourage them.

4. 2 Timothy 4:12: Tychicus is mentioned briefly in this passage, where Paul informs Timothy that he has sent Tychicus to Ephesus.

From these passages, it's evident that Tychicus was highly regarded by Paul and entrusted with important responsibilities in his ministry. He served as a messenger, bearer of letters, and encourager to various Christian communities, demonstrating his dedication and commitment to spreading the Gospel.

7. Carpus - Carpus is mentioned only once in the New Testament, in 2 Timothy 4:13, where the apostle Paul writes, "When you come, bring the cloak that I left with Carpus at Troas, also the books, and above all the parchments."

From this brief mention, it's understood that Carpus was an individual residing in the city of Troas. Paul left some personal belongings with him, including a cloak, books, and parchments. Unfortunately, beyond this single mention, the New Testament does not provide further information about Carpus or his role in the early Christian community. As a result, little else is known about him.

8. Alexander - In 2 Timothy 4:14-15, the apostle Paul mentions an individual named Alexander:

"Alexander the coppersmith did me great harm; the Lord will repay him according to his deeds. Beware of him yourself, for he strongly opposed our message."

This passage suggests that Alexander was someone who caused harm to Paul, likely by opposing his teachings or mission. The specific identity of this Alexander is uncertain, as there were likely many individuals with that name during that time. Some scholars speculate that he could have been a prominent opponent of Christianity in the community where Paul was writing to Timothy.

Given the context, it's evident that Alexander was viewed negatively by Paul, who warned Timothy to be cautious around him. However, beyond this mention in 2 Timothy, the New Testament doesn't provide further details about this individual.

9. Pricsa/Priscilla - Priscilla, also known as Prisca, was a prominent figure in the early Christian church, mentioned several times in the New Testament. She, along with her husband Aquila, played a significant role in spreading the Christian message and supporting various early Christian communities.

Priscilla is mentioned in the following passages:

1. Acts 18:2, 18, 26: Priscilla and Aquila are introduced as a Jewish couple who were tentmakers by trade. They had been living in Rome but were expelled from the city along with other Jews by Emperor Claudius. They met the apostle Paul in Corinth and became close associates, working alongside him in tentmaking.

2. Romans 16:3-5: Paul sends greetings to Priscilla and Aquila, commending them for risking their lives for him and stating that all the churches of the Gentiles are grateful to them. This passage indicates their significant contributions to the early Christian movement.

3. 1 Corinthians 16:19: Paul mentions that Priscilla and Aquila are hosting a church in their house and sends greetings to them.

4. 2 Timothy 4:19: In the closing remarks of this letter, Paul sends greetings to Priscilla and Aquila, indicating that they were still active in their support of the Christian community.

Priscilla and Aquila are often mentioned together, indicating their partnership in ministry and their close relationship with Paul. They are portrayed as hospitable, supportive, and dedicated to the spread of the Christian faith. Their example highlights the important role of laypersons in the early church and the significance of partnerships in ministry.

10. Aquila - Aquila, also known as Aquilas, was a prominent figure in the early Christian church, mentioned several times in the New Testament. He was the husband of Priscilla, and together they played a significant role in spreading the Christian message and supporting various early Christian communities.

Aquila is mentioned in the following passages:

1. Acts 18:2, 18, 26: Aquila and Priscilla are introduced as a Jewish couple who were tentmakers by trade. They had been living in Rome but were expelled from the city along with other Jews by Emperor Claudius. They met the apostle Paul in Corinth and became close associates, working alongside him in tentmaking.

2. Romans 16:3-5: Paul sends greetings to Aquila and Priscilla, commending them for risking their lives for him and stating that all the churches of the Gentiles are grateful to them. This passage indicates their significant contributions to the early Christian movement.

3. 1 Corinthians 16:19: Paul mentions that Aquila and Priscilla are hosting a church in their house and sends greetings to them.

4. 2 Timothy 4:19: In the closing remarks of this letter, Paul sends greetings to Aquila and Priscilla, indicating that they were still active in their support of the Christian community.

Aquila and Priscilla are often mentioned together, indicating their partnership in ministry and their close relationship with Paul. They are portrayed as hospitable, supportive, and dedicated to the spread of the Christian faith. Their example highlights the important role of laypersons in the early church and the significance of partnerships in ministry.

11. Onesiphorus - Onesiphorus is mentioned in the New Testament in the letters of Paul, specifically in 2 Timothy 1:16-18 and 2 Timothy 4:19.

In 2 Timothy 1:16-18, Paul writes:

"May the Lord grant mercy to the household of Onesiphorus, for he often refreshed me and was not ashamed of my chains, but when he arrived in Rome he searched for me earnestly and found me— may the Lord grant him to find mercy from the Lord on that day!—and you well know all the service he rendered at Ephesus."

This passage indicates that Onesiphorus was a supporter of Paul, even when Paul was imprisoned. He showed kindness and care for Paul, seeking him out and providing assistance.

In 2 Timothy 4:19, Paul writes:

"Greet Prisca and Aquila, and the household of Onesiphorus."

Here, Onesiphorus is mentioned in the context of sending greetings to him and his household, indicating that he was part of the Christian community and known to Paul.

Although not much more is known about Onesiphorus beyond these passages, he is remembered as an example of faithfulness, kindness, and support within the early Christian community.

12. Erastus - Erastus is mentioned in the New Testament in three verses, all written by the apostle Paul:

1. Romans 16:23: "Gaius, whose hospitality I and the whole church here enjoy, sends you his greetings. Erastus, who is the city's director of public works, and our brother Quartus send you their greetings."

2. 2 Timothy 4:20: "Erastus stayed in Corinth, and I left Trophimus sick in Miletus."

3. Acts 19:22: "He sent two of his helpers, Timothy and Erastus, to Macedonia, while he stayed in the province of Asia a little longer."

From these passages, it is understood that Erastus held a significant position in the city of Corinth, serving as the director of public works. He was also a trusted associate of Paul, being sent on missions and sending greetings to fellow believers. However, beyond these mentions, the New Testament does not provide further details about Erastus or his role in the early Christian community.

13. Trophimus - Trophimus is mentioned in several verses in the New Testament, primarily in the writings of the apostle Paul:

1. Acts 20:4: "He was accompanied by Sopater son of Pyrrhus from Berea, Aristarchus and Secundus from Thessalonica, Gaius from Derbe, Timothy also, and Tychicus and Trophimus from the province of Asia."

2. Acts 21:29: "For they had previously seen Trophimus the Ephesian with him in the city, and they supposed that Paul had brought him into the temple."

3. 2 Timothy 4:20: "Erastus stayed in Corinth, and I left Trophimus sick in Miletus."

From these passages, it's evident that Trophimus was a companion and fellow worker of the apostle Paul. He is described as being from the province of Asia and was likely part of the early Christian community there. Trophimus accompanied Paul on his journeys and was known to be with him during his travels to Jerusalem. In the last mention in 2 Timothy, it appears that Trophimus fell ill, and Paul left him in Miletus while continuing his journey.

14. Eubulus - Eubulus is mentioned only once in the New Testament, in 2 Timothy 4:21, where the apostle Paul writes:

"Do your best to come before winter. Eubulus sends greetings to you, as do Pudens and Linus and Claudia and all the brothers."

From this passage, it is understood that Eubulus was among those who sent greetings to Timothy, likely indicating that he was a member of the Christian community known to Timothy or Paul. However, beyond this mention, the

New Testament does not provide further details about Eubulus or his role in the early Christian community.

15. Pudens - is mentioned in the New Testament in 2 Timothy 4:21, where the apostle Paul writes:

"Do your best to come before winter. Eubulus sends greetings to you, as do Pudens and Linus and Claudia and all the brothers."

From this passage, it appears that Pudens was someone known to Timothy and was among those sending greetings to him. However, beyond this mention, the New Testament does not provide further details about Pudens or his role in the early Christian community.

Outside of the New Testament, there are references to a "Pudens" in early Christian writings and Roman history. However, it's uncertain whether any of these references correspond to the Pudens mentioned by Paul.

16. Linus - Linus is mentioned in the New Testament in 2 Timothy 4:21, where the apostle Paul writes:

"Do your best to come before winter. Eubulus sends greetings to you, as do Pudens and Linus and Claudia and all the brothers."

From this passage, it appears that Linus was someone known to Timothy and was among those sending greetings to him. However, beyond this mention, the New Testament does not provide further details about Linus or his role in the early Christian community.

Traditionally, Linus has been identified as one of the early bishops of Rome, with some Christian traditions considering him to be the immediate successor to the apostle Peter as bishop of Rome. However, historical evidence for this is scarce, and it is largely based on later Christian tradition rather than explicit biblical or contemporary historical records.

17. Claudia - Claudia is mentioned in the New Testament in 2 Timothy 4:21, where the apostle Paul writes:

"Do your best to come before winter. Eubulus sends greetings to you, as do Pudens and Linus and Claudia and all the brothers."

From this passage, it seems that Claudia was someone known to Timothy and was among those sending greetings to him. However, beyond this mention, the New Testament does not provide further details about Claudia or her role in the early Christian community.

The name Claudia was fairly common in the Roman world, so it's challenging to determine the specific identity of the Claudia mentioned by Paul. Some speculate that she might have been a believer or supporter of the Christian faith, while others suggest she might have been someone associated with the Roman aristocracy. However, without additional information, it's difficult to ascertain her precise identity or significance.

Biblical Locations

1. Thessalonica

2. Galatia

3. Dalmatia

4. Ephesus

5. Troas

6. Corinth

7. Miletus

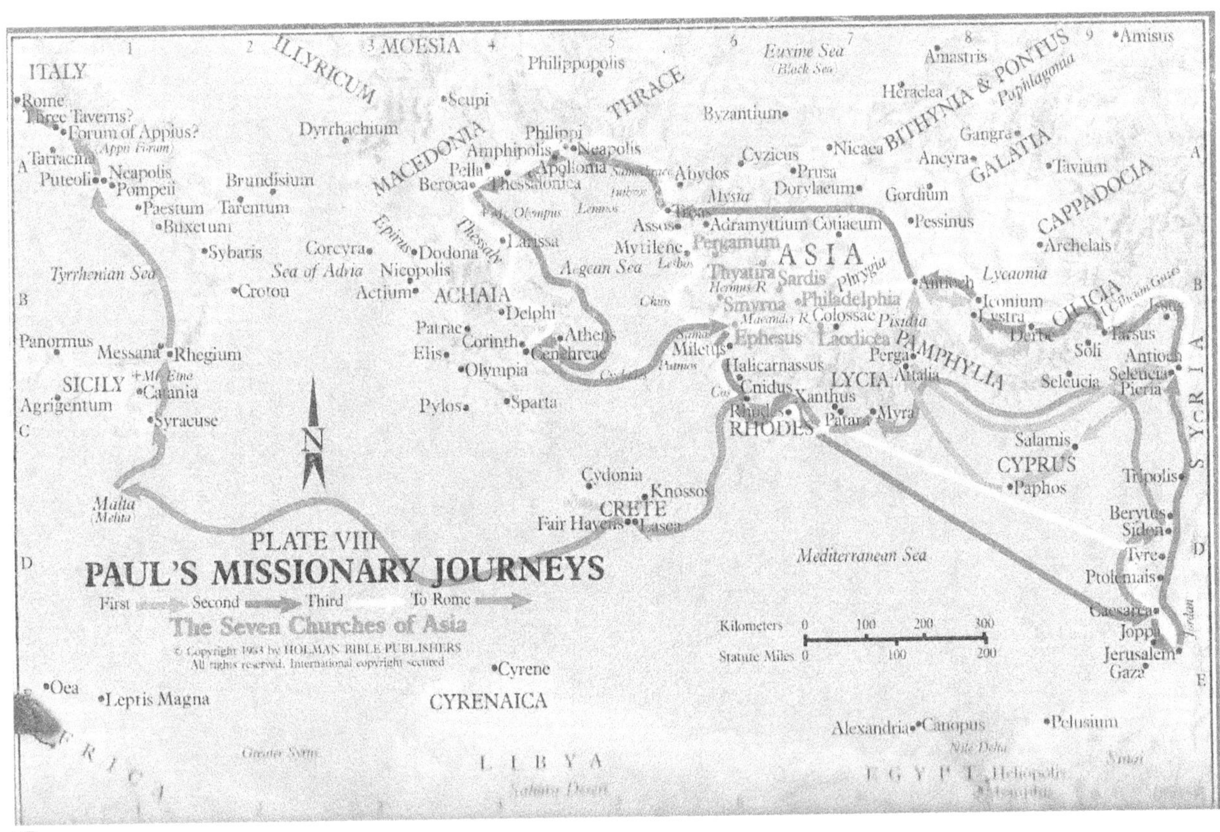

---

[17] 1. Author
Mooney
Mooney
Patrick
Patrick Mooney is a 34-year secondary English teaching vetera, Patrick
Patrick Mooney is a 34-year secondary English teaching veteran in
Northern California with a bachelor's in English and a master's in secondary education. Besides serving as an
English, and Patrick Mooney, "Asia Menor Na Bíblia," EDUCA, accessed March 4, 2024,
https://w20.b2m.cz/post/asia-menor-na-biblia.html.

Thoughts

Leaving a church because the new pastor is saying things you do not want to hear can show a resistance to new ideas. Paul was extremely concerned about other expressions of Christianity. Taking into account all the different possibilities today, can one say Paul got everything correct?

Biblography

"5. Paul in Macedonia (Acts 15:36-18:22, 49-50 AD)." 5. Paul in Macedonia (Acts 15:36-18:22, 49-50 AD) -- Apostle Paul: Passsionate Discipleship. Accessed February 28, 2024. https://www.jesuswalk.com/paul/05_macedonia.htm.

Author   Patrick Mooney   Patrick Mooney is a 34-year secondary English teaching vetera, Patrick Mooney   Patrick Mooney is a 34-year secondary English teaching veteran in Northern California with a bachelor's in English and a master's in secondary education. Besides serving as an English, and Patrick Mooney. "Asia Menor Na Bíblia." EDUCA. Accessed March 4, 2024. https://w20.b2m.cz/post/asia-menor-na-biblia.html.

byAdministrator, Posted. "Paul's First Missionary Journey." Bible Mapper Atlas, January 15, 2024. https://biblemapper.com/blog/index.php/2020/02/13/southern-galatia/.

Errico, Rocco A., and George M. Lamsa. *Aramaic light on Galatians through hebrews: A commentary based on Aramaic, the language of jesus, and ancient near eastern customs.* Smyma, GA: Noohra Foundation, 2005.

GotQuestions.org. "Home." GotQuestions.org, May 11, 2017. https://www.gotquestions.org/Lois-and-Eunice.html.

Hymenaeus - Encyclopedia of the bible - bible gateway. Accessed February 19, 2024. https://www.biblegateway.com/resources/encyclopedia-of-the-bible/Hymenaeus.

Jannes and jambres - encyclopedia of the bible - bible gateway. Accessed February 28, 2024. https://www.biblegateway.com/resources/encyclopedia-of-the-bible/Jannes-Jambres.

"Onesiphorus." Wikipedia, January 31, 2024. https://en.wikipedia.org/wiki/Onesiphorus.

"Paul and Barnabas in Lystra and Derbe :: Paul and Barnabas Visit Lystra and Derbe (Acts 14:8-28)." FreeBibleimages. Accessed February 28, 2024. https://freebibleimages.org/illustrations/paul-lystra-derbe/.

"Philetus (Biblical Figure)." Wikipedia, September 19, 2021.
    https://en.wikipedia.org/wiki/Philetus_(biblical_figure).

Topical bible: Hermogenes. Accessed February 11, 2024.
    https://biblehub.com/topical/h/hermogenes.htm.

Topical bible: Phygellus. Accessed February 11, 2024.
    https://biblehub.com/topical/p/phygellus.htm.

Webmaster, GES. "Secure yet Scrutinized – 2 Timothy 2:11-13." Grace Evangelical
    Society, September 1, 1988. https://faithalone.org/journal-articles/secure-yet-
    scrutinized-2-timothy-211-13/.